Act and Being

Act and Being

*Towards a Theology of
the Divine Attributes*

Colin E. Gunton

scm press

British Library Cataloguing in Publication data

A catalogue record for this book is available
from the British Library

0 334 02892 2

First published in 2002 by SCM Press
9-17 St Albans Place, London N1 0NX

www.scm-canterburypress.co.uk

SCM Press is a division of
SCM-Canterbury Press Ltd

Printed and bound in Great Britain by
Creative Print and Design, Wales

Contents

Preface

This rather rapidly written book is a revision and expansion of four public lectures given by invitation at Multnomah Bible College and Multnomah Biblical Seminary, Portland Oregon. I am grateful for the invitation and for the kind hospitality of the institution during our visit, and would mention especially Paul Metzger and Ronald Frost. The lectures were intended originally to serve as a draft theology of the divine attributes, and so to contribute to an extended treatment of the doctrine of God in a projected systematic theology. However, as my dissatisfaction with the way this topic has often been treated increased, a more critical drive took over, so that this short book is more an attempt at ground-breaking than an account of the attributes, although the book does close with some outline suggestions. I hope that an extended account may eventually follow in their train. The burden of the critique is perhaps predictable: that much of our inherited doctrine appears to owe too little to biblical and trinitarian considerations, too much to a priori philosophical decision about what God may be conceived not to be. But the exploration brought to light many more positive features: that scripture has its own critique of pagan polytheism, and it is far more satisfactory than that of the negative way; that traditional treatments of the divine attributes depend far too much on the shaky support of biblical proof-texts taken out of context; that there is much to be said on biblical grounds for John Duns Scotus' doctrine of univocity; and that exploration of the distinctive attributes of the particular persons of the Trinity has much to teach us.

As always in these circumstances there are many people to thank. I owe to Alex Wright formerly of the SCM Press yet another debt of gratitude for encouraging a project which otherwise may well have gone unrealized; and to my daughter Carolyn once for again taking from me the burden of proof reading and the preparation of the index. Members of the Research Institute in Systematic Theology heard and discussed the lectures in a number of special seminars, and, as always, contributed much to the process of writing and revision. Two members of the Institute require special mention. Rufus Burton's research into the theology of the holiness of God not only provided many references and much food for thought, but also helped to bring to realization what is perhaps the central burden of this study: that the absence before the Reformation of any serious treatment of God's holiness, which has some claim to be at the very centre of a biblical account of the divine attributes, is a symptom of the sheer inadequacy of traditional treatments of this central topic. It is appropriate that I should also be able to thank Rufus's parents, Rufus and Mary, whose generous hospitality helped to make my and my wife's visit to Oregon so memorable. The second to be mentioned is Shirley Martin, who not only chaired the special seminars but devoted many hours to reading and discussing with me the details of the book. Indeed, the crucial final chapter was sketched out in conversation with her, so that it is no exaggeration to say that this is in some measure her book also.

Colin Gunton
King's College, London
August 2002

I

A Hybrid Deity?

I The Situation Addressed

To speak of God's attributes is to attempt to speak of the kind of god that God is; of the things that characterize him as God; of what makes him to be God, rather than some other being or kind of being. While the doctrine of the Trinity, we might say, identifies God, says who he is, as Father, Son and Spirit, the doctrine of the attributes is a proposal about the defining characteristics of the deity. To be sure, this is not an absolute distinction, and one cannot be divorced from the other. To speak of the Trinity is already to say something of God's characteristics, while to speak of the attributes apart from the Trinity – as is often done – is a mistake, and one which we shall be exploring below. The central difficulty of the situation as it meets us after nearly two thousand years of discussion is that there seems to be little clarity about how the two are related: how the identity of God as Father, Son and Holy Spirit relates to the kind of things that have been, and are, said of the kind of being that God is.

II Aspects of the Historical Background

The Fathers are often ambivalent, indeed sometimes apparently in two different minds, in their attitude to the Greek
philosophical heritage in the context of which they did
much of their thinking. On the one hand, the philosophers
and their works are excoriated as the source of all ills, and
not only by those, like Tertullian, who accuse them of being
the fount of heresy.[1] Clement of Alexandria provides a
more illuminating study. Robert Jenson has recently drawn
attention to the fact that a positive reference to Plato comes
after 'chapters of invective against the Greek-taught pagans
for their worship of God's works instead of God', where
Clement writes: 'I long for God, not the works of God.
Now – whom from among you can I take for a co-worker
in this longing . . . ? Perhaps Plato . . . '[2] The outcome of this
ambivalence, aspects of which will be traced in this study,
is, especially so far as the doctrine of God is concerned, a
deep fissure running, often unrecognized, through the body
of Christian teaching. This will be argued to be particularly
easily recognized in the theologians who write in the aftermath of the Reformation, because there the new emphasis
on a doctrine of God derived from the biblical narrative
is uneasily combined with antithetical doctrines deeply
sedimented in the tradition. That is to say, the Christian
doctrine of God is for much of its history a hybrid of two
organisms.

Hybrids come in many forms, from those that represent

---

[1] Tertullian, *Praescr.*, 7.
[2] Robert W. Jenson, *Systematic Theology*, volume 1, *The Triune
God*; volume 2, *The Works of God* (New York and Oxford: Oxford
University Press, 1997, 1999), vol. 1, p. 10, citing *Exhortation to the
Greeks*, vi. 59.

a new, stronger and more fruitful development to those which are in some way merely dull or even monstrous. There are many varying estimates of the character of the deity which emerged when Greece and Jerusalem cross-pollinated one another, and, indeed, many different variations on the combination. We shall meet some of the different forms and judgments in the pages which are to come. But there is one feature of the developments which needs to be faced and, I believe, rejected. It is one of the tragedies – one could almost say crimes – of Christian theological history that the Old Testament was effectively displaced by Greek philosophy as the theological basis of the doctrine of God, certainly so far as the doctrine of the divine attributes is concerned. Eric Osborn's comment, that 'The first Greek steps towards a Christian view of God were unwittingly indicated by Xenophanes of Colophon . . .',[3] might have a grain of truth in it, but of greater moment is the fact that this appears to have had more effect than the steps towards, indeed articulation of, an essentially Christian view of God which is already present in the Old Testament. The irony of Osborn's observation is that he made it in a book on Irenaeus, who, despite all the echoes of the Greek position, made it his business to stress again and again that Christ is to be found in the pages of the Old Testament scriptures. And while it is not the case that the Old Testament was explicitly downgraded by the tradition in favour of philosophy, there is a tendency to say that the latter achieves for the Gentiles the equivalent of what the Old Testament does for the Jews:

Perchance, too, philosophy was given to the Greeks

---

[3] Eric Osborn, *Irenaeus of Lyons* (Cambridge: Cambridge University Press, 2001), p. 34.

directly and primarily, till the Lord should call the Greeks.
For this was a schoolmaster to bring 'the Hellenic mind,'
as the law [was for] the Hebrews, 'to Christ'. Philosophy,
therefore, was a preparation, paving the way for him
who is perfected in Christ.[4]

In that passage, the Old Testament is implicitly downgraded
in two ways: narrowed in its function (it is important for
the New Testament far more than is suggested by the one
allusion to a saying of Paul to be found there) and relativ-
ized by being reduced, at least in this respect, to an equality
of function with the philosophy of the Greeks. The distortion finds its way into the mainstream Western tradition; in
the words contained in the Requiem *Teste David et Sybilla*
we encounter a juxtaposition in parallel of Old Testament
and pagan philosophy, which surely should not be.

The tendency to make a particular philosophical tradition definitive for Christian theology is still to be observed,
most recently in the 1998 papal encyclical on faith and
reason. While it can be conceded to the Holy Father that 'in
engaging great cultures [sc. that of India] for the first time,
the Church cannot abandon what she has gained from her
inculturation in the world of Greco-Latin thought',[5] she
must surely abandon what she has *mistakenly* taken, as will
appear later. And the point is this: it is often enough
remarked these days that the centuries-long neglect of the
Old Testament has served to the detriment of the Christian
faith, nowhere better illustrated than by the long history of
anti-Semitism, but more generally in the impoverishment of
our grasp of the breadth and depth of the gospel's meaning.
This is no more truly the case than in the treatment of the

[4] Clement of Alexandria, *Stromata*, 1. 5.
[5] *Encyclical Letter Fides et Ratio of the Supreme Pontiff John Paul II
on the Relation between Faith and Reason* (Vatican City, 1998), §72.

being of God, that most central of doctrines. Evidence will be offered in the following chapters that this has been deeply paganized, so that nineteenth-century jibes about Christianity as Platonism for the masses are not so far off the mark. The key to the matter is to be found in the location of the divine in a realm that is in some way opposed to or the negation of this world, and we shall find evidence for that in the most orthodox of theologians. So much of the modern rejection of Christianity derives from a reaction against that, which is so widespread that it cannot be ignored as misrepresentation, misrepresentation though it often contains in plenty. The treatment of the divine attributes over time provides a prime example of this tendency to an essentially sub-Christian doctrine of God, as we shall see.

Underlying the papal defence we have met of the indispensability of the Greek contribution to theology is a conviction that the teaching of the Christian faith, dependent as it is on particularities, requires foundation in a general philosophy of being. However, the attempt to supplement the particular by the general runs the risk – and, indeed, historically it is more than a risk, even a fact – that the particular will be constrained or even overwhelmed by the general. Moreover, the supposition that one particular philosophy – for that is in effect what is being claimed – is necessary for Christian theology is an odd one, and has been decisively refuted by Robert Jenson. He points out that Greek philosophy and its descendants have no more claim to universality than any other set of doctrines. The various accounts of the structure of being in the Presocratic and classical Greek philosophies are in point of fact *theologies*, attempts to conceive the world in relation to the divine. '[T]his body of theology was as historically particular as any other set of historical proposals: it comprised part of the theology that Greek religious thinkers, pondering the revelations claimed for Homer and Parmenides, had provided for the cults of Mediterranean antiquity . . . '[6] As we shall see, Greek philosophy begins as an attempt not only to reject the inadequate gods of popular belief but to provide a rational version of the ancient world-view those gods represent. It is a demythologization (*Aufhebung?*) only as a translation or transposition, not a displacement or abolition. It is when Christian theology becomes dependent on the philosophers' speculations rather than on the equivalent Old Testament polemics against paganism that the troubles begin. In that light, we must move to another salient characteristic of our intellectual world.

III Aspects of the Intellectual Situation

In the next chapter, we shall review some of the chief problems facing those who would essay a doctrine of the divine attributes. As an introduction to this, let us examine the problem of problems, that which dominates all treatment of the subject. This is that we think that we know what the attributes are. 'By the name God I understand a substance that is infinite [eternal, immutable], independent, all-knowing, all-powerful, and by which I myself and everything else . . . have been created.'[7] Similar definitions can be found, especially in text books on the philosophy of religion. But let me pause a little longer over the theology of Charles Hodge, and two citations. The first appears early in the first part of his *Systematic Theology*, entitled, 'Theology Proper'.

---

[6] Jenson, *Systematic Theology*, vol. 1, p. 7.
[7] René Descartes, *Meditation 3*.

Theism is the doctrine of an extra-mundane, personal God, the creator, preserver and governor of the world.[8]

The second, which I shall cite at greater length, appears about 150 pages later:

Probably the best definition of God ever penned by man, is that given in the 'Westminster Catechism': 'God is a Spirit, infinite, eternal, and unchangeable, in his being, wisdom, power, holiness, justice, goodness, and truth.' This is a true definition; for it states the class of beings to which God is to be referred. He is Spirit; and He is distinguished from all other spirits in that He is infinite, eternal and unchangeable in his being and perfections. It is also a complete definition, in so far as it is an exhaustive statement of the contents of our idea of God.[9]

It is not that we should necessarily want to deny the attribution of most of the qualities to God; nor is it that I am unaware of the fact that Hodge delimits carefully what he means by definition and that he has elsewhere much more to say about God. It is rather a matter of what is left out, and particularly what Robert Letham has recently pointed out, that Hodge 'does not get around to suggesting that God is triune until after 250 pages of detailed exposition of the doctrine of God'.[10] Of theological dissatisfaction with this, volumes could be written.

[8] Charles Hodge, *Systematic Theology* (Grand Rapids: Eerdmans, 1989 (1871–3)), vol. 1, p. 204.
[9] Hodge, *Systematic Theology*, vol. 1, p. 367.
[10] He continues: 'and then tell me exactly how that can help us in our encounter with Islam'. Review of Colin E. Gunton, *The Triune Creator*, *Westminster Theological Journal* 62 (2000), page numbers are not known.

As the argument of this book proceeds, we shall find that
there are many far less satisfactory attempted definitions
than that of Hodge. But the point remains, that theologians
often appear to have been content, certainly in the first
instance, with a list of apparently intelligible and often
rather abstract terms as 'the contents of our idea of God'.
And it is against the over-confidence with which Hodge
claims to provide the 'exhaustive statement' that the
moments of truth in an otherwise badly construed doctrine,
that of the unknowability or incomprehensibility of God,
are to be found. We shall, then, approach the topic with
an initial theory or hypothesis in mind and test its truth
especially in the third and fourth chapters: that so far as the
divine attributes are concerned, the doctrine has often been
approached using the wrong method; developing the
wrong content; and even when that has not been entirely
the case, treating things in the wrong order. As we shall see,
this has much to do with what has become the tangled web
of the relations between what can broadly be identified as
the Greek and Hebrew determinants of the topic, but, as it
is indeed a tangled web, we must attempt to disentangle
the threads as individually and carefully as is possible. But
this must be prefaced by some remarks about terminology.

There are three terms with which, from the beginning, we
must become acquainted. The first is the one we have met,
'attribute'. As Karl Barth has pointed out, this is a problematic term. When something is attributed to something or
someone, such as certain characteristics – for example, as
was said recently of a British politician that he is 'the master
of the non-denial denial' – it might be done because it is the
case, or because it is believed to be true, or because it is
wished that the thing or person be seen in that way. The
case of political abuse is a perfect example of the difference.

The stress in the latter case is on what the human mind does, ascribing certain characteristics to the object of its attribution. That puts the emphasis the wrong way round. We are concerned, rather, first of all with who God is, not what we attribute to him, and it was for a reason similar to this that Barth preferred – and this is our second term – the word 'perfections', 'because it points at once to the thing itself instead of merely to its formal aspect, and because instead of something general it expresses at once that which is clearly distinctive'.[11] This seems to be right: what we seek are not our attributions but the ways in which God is perfect. Theology, as Barth knew, is the discipline which seeks, so far as God grants and it can achieve, to bring to speech in many different ways the perfection of God, so that he can be known, praised and obeyed. It is not a matter of what *we attribute*, but of what he *reveals himself* to be. It is because of his relentless pursuit of this matter that Barth's treatment of the divine perfections is one of the finest accounts of the topic to be found in theological history, although some criticisms of it will be in a later chapter. Nevertheless, because it accords well with familiar usage, I shall maintain the traditional language of the attributes, hoping to keep in mind that we are concerned only with what God grants us to attribute to him on the basis of what he has shown us.

A similar confusion arises in connection with the third term we meet in the tradition, that of the divine names. As we review the history of our topic, it becomes clear that an important distinction can be drawn, and it is parallel to that we have met between perfection and attribute. It is

[11] Karl Barth, *Church Dogmatics*, translation edited by G. W. Bromiley and T. F. Torrance (Edinburgh: T. & T. Clark, 1957–1975), 2/1, p. 322.

between the notion of a revealed name and the terms in which some theologians and philosophers have spoken of how we name God. Here our best illustration is to be found in the opposing ways in which a text of scripture is interpreted. All comes to a head in the different ways in which Exodus 3.13f. and similar passages in the Old Testament speak of the matter:

> Moses said to God, 'Suppose I go to the Israelites and say to them, "The God of your fathers has sent me to you," and they ask me, "What is his name?" Then what shall I tell them?'
>
> God said to Moses, 'I AM WHO I AM. This is what you are to say to the Israelites: "I AM has sent me to you."' (Exod. 3.13f.)

From quite early times, particularly after the work of the fifth-century Pseudo-Dionysius, it came to be held that this 'I am' means that God's primary name is that of Being. John of Damascus puts it thus:

> It appears then that the most proper of all the names given to God is 'He that is,' as He Himself said in answer to Moses on the mountain . . . For He keeps all being in His own embrace, like a sea of essence, infinite and unseen.[12]

As we shall see in a later chapter, such exegesis comes to form the basis of the tradition of negative theology, of naming God in terms of what he is not. The tradition is surely justified in part: in seeing here the basis of the need to limit carefully what our words can claim to describe of God's 'inner being', if we can so speak. As Brevard Childs

[12] John of Damascus, *De Fide Orth.*, 1. 9.

comments, '[t]he formula is paradoxically both an answer and a refusal of an answer'.[13] We shall see later in the book that a similar point can be made about the Second Isaiah's apparent adoption of negative theology in the well-known passage in chapter 40. And yet, to the sceptical observer John's exposition seems more a piece of Platonic abstraction than a true exegesis of the biblical text.

There are two reasons for this. First is that there is a case for translating the expression in the future tense: 'I will be who I will be . . .', which makes its reference to God as a 'sea of being' more than questionable. 'God announces that his intentions will be revealed in his future acts, which he now refuses to explain.'[14] Second, the expression is glossed by the writer as referring to 'the God of Abraham, the God of Isaac and the God of Jacob', a somewhat clear instance of naming. God hides himself while naming himself, but he does give us a name, an actual description, albeit one which has to be filled out in future historical acts. It is surely significant that the biblical texts that take up the reference appeal not to 'being', but to the name revealed in historical action. 'I am the God of your fathers, the God of Abraham, Isaac and Jacob.' (Significantly, that is the part of the divine address which is cited by Stephen in Acts 7.32.) On the one hand, we appear to be given a biblical basis for one of the traditional divine attributes, God's aseity, that he has his being in and for himself, quite apart from our knowing and naming him; and, on the other, that the nature of this aseity is not left to us to determine philosophically, but is revealed biblically through God's acts in time and history.

There is our topic in a nutshell. What is the relation

---

[13] Brevard S. Childs, *Exodus. A Commentary* (London: SCM Press, 1974), p. 76.
[14] Childs, *Exodus*, p. 76.

between the tradition of the divine names which we meet in Pseudo-Dionysius and his successors, a tradition we shall meet again and again, and the apparently more naive belief that God is primarily to be named – because he so names himself – as the God of Abraham, Isaac and Jacob and then as the Father of our Lord Jesus Christ, who by raising him from the dead has given him the name that is above every name? What, that is to say, is the relation between a metaphysic of being in which God is named by what is essentially a method of philosophical abstraction and the biblical phenomenon of the revealed name? In the next section, a brief account of what the former method is will be attempted.

IV God as Cause

One of the most acute observers of the nature of the traditional doctrine of the attributes is Friedrich Schleiermacher:

> Now we may remark concerning these methods that there are three accepted ways of arriving at the divine attributes – the way of removal of limits (*via eminentiae*), the way of negation or denial (*via negationis*), and the way of causality (*via causalitatis*).

We may observe in passing that such methods are largely philosophical, in the respect that they can work in abstraction from the biblical narrative. They are *cosmological*, in being read off, so to speak, the observed or intuited features of the world quite apart from any particular initiative of God in relation to it. But that is not the main point to be noted about Schleiermacher's perceptiveness. Noting that the first two methods cannot operate on their own, he rightly concludes that the third method is in a sense basic, because 'all the divine attributes to be dealt with in Christian Dogmatics must somehow go back to the divine causality . . .'[15]

Where Schleiermacher is particularly perceptive is in realizing that causality is at the heart of the matter. The root of the threefold method of negation, eminence and causality is to be found in the discussions of Greek philosophy after Plato about how a purely spiritual divinity can be conceived to give rise to material reality. The problem for us – to take up a point made in section II above – lies in the almost universal (dualist) assumption of the opposition of the material to the spiritual or intellectual which appears to underlie this method. Plato's fragmentary treatment of the various ways in which the forms might be supposed to be causes – a multivalent concept in Plato – gave rise to attempts to conceive more clearly how the experienced universe, a combination as it apparently was of the intelligible and the sensible, might flow from – and metaphors of emanation are recurrent – the being of the purely intellectual. Lacking the kind of concept of personal divine action that became possible only in the light of scripture, and in any case associating particular divine action with the

---

[15] F. D. E. Schleiermacher, *The Christian Faith*, translated by H. R. Mackintosh and J. S. Stewart (Edinburgh: T. & T. Clark, 1928), pp. 197f. I have omitted the final clause, because it reveals the feature which is peculiar to Schleiermacher's own treatment of experienced rather than metaphysically posited causality, the chief difference between his and the classical Thomist account, which we shall be meeting from time to time. It is quite a difference however, Schleiermacher's 'since they [the attributes] are only meant to explain the feeling of absolute dependence' referring to feeling, while for Aquinas, the patterns of causality are meant to explain the structures of reality. Whether they result in a more satisfactory doctrine of God is something we shall be examining.

anthropomorphic antics of the gods of Greek poetry, the later Greeks took refuge in analogy. By this is meant a theory not primarily of language, of how ordinary words could be shown to speak of the divine, but of being. Particularly clear in Plotinus is an account of hierarchically graded being, from the purely intellectual at the summit, to brute and unformed matter at the foot. Proclus' similar account is described by Copleston as follows:

> There must be . . . a First Cause, whence the multiplicity of beings proceed 'As branches from a root', some being nearer to the First Cause, others more remote. Moreover, there can only be one such First Cause, for the existence of a multiplicity is always secondary to unity. This must exist since we are logically compelled to refer all multiplicity back to unity. . . . It follows that we are really not entitled to predicate anything positively of the ultimate Principle: we can only say what it is *not*, realising that it stands above all discursive thought and positive predication, ineffable and incomprehensible.[16]

Is this in essence any different from what Schleiermacher feels that he must say about God, *mutatis mutandis*? 'All attributes which we ascribe to God are to be taken not as something special in God, but only something special in the manner in which the feeling of absolute dependence is to be related to him.'[17]

The credit, if that be the word, for introducing this tradition of negative theology into Christian theology must go chiefly to Pseudo-Dionysius, mistakenly given authority

---

[16] Frederick Copleston, *A History of Philosophy*, volume 1, *Greece and Rome* (Westminster, Maryland: The Newman Press, 1966), p. 479.
[17] Schleiermacher, *The Christian Faith*, heading to §50, p. 194.

in the tradition because it was long believed that he was the one who listened to Paul's speech on the Areopagus recorded in Acts 17. Dionysius' treatment of *The Divine Names* is marked by a number of features which will set the scene for the critique of the traditional doctrine of the attributes which is essayed in this book. Let me begin with what can be called the symptoms of an underlying disease. The first is that although scripture is quoted and alluded to liberally, reference to the revealed names of the deity are, so far as I can see, totally absent. The 'names' which are treated are abstractions: goodness, beauty, being, and the like. To be sure, these and such concepts are rightly attributable to God; what is crucial is what they mean, and whether their pedigree is essentially Neoplatonic rather than biblical. A second symptom is a similar ignoring of particular divine actions, with the exception of the most general appeal to dogmatic christology. There are indeed at least two places where the text is distorted by the exclusion of christology, both of them references to Colossians 1.17: 'in him [Christ] all things hold together'. In both cases, the text is made to refer to God *simpliciter*, and rendered impersonal. 'It is there "before all things and in it all things hold together".'[18] A third symptom is the apparently modalist, or nearly modalist, doctrine of the Trinity which is taught, with its clear stress on the priority of God's oneness over his tri-unity:

> And so all these scriptural utterances celebrate the supreme Deity by describing it [*sic*] as a monad or henad, because of its supernatural simplicity and indivisible

[18] Pseudo-Dionysius, *The Divine Names*, 593D. The translation is from *Pseudo-Dionysius. The Complete Works*, translated by Colm Luibheid (London: SPCK, 1987), p. 54. See also 700A, p. 75.

unity . . . They also describe it as a Trinity, for with a
transcendent fecundity it is manifested as 'three persons'.[19]

That the unity of God might *consist in* the threeness of
the persons rather than lying above them never appears to
have occurred to this writer, but this tendency to modalism
is typical of Pseudo-Dionysius' position.

For our purposes, however, the chief point to observe in
Dionysius is the elevation of timeless, metaphysical causality
over the temporally and economically structured biblical
characterizations of God's action in the world. Few pages
of *The Divine Names* pass without some use of the notion
of God as cause, and two examples will at least suggest that
the conception is Neoplatonic and analogical rather than
biblical. The problem is not that many of the things that
Pseudo-Dionysius says cannot be said, but that the way
they are qualified appears to take them out of a realm in
which God is made known in his action in and towards the
world. The problem is a relentless concentration on what
God is not, on the analogically reached doctrine that God is
essentially what the world is not.

> The God who is transcends everything by virtue of his
> power. He is the substantive Cause and maker of being,
> subsistence, of existence, of substance, and of nature. . . .
> He is the reality beneath time and the eternity behind
> being. . . . He was not. He will not be. He did not come
> to be. He is not in the midst of becoming. He will not
> come to be. No. He is not. Rather, he is the essence of
> being for the things which have being.[20]

[19] Pseudo-Dionysius, *The Divine Names*, 589D, Luibheid, p. 51. The
'it' seems to be a translator's decision, but if it represents an accurate
rendering of the author's meaning, it is evidence for an impersonal deity
underlying the persons and rendering Dionysius' trinitarianism modalistic.
[20] Pseudo-Dionysius, *The Divine Names*, 817D, Luibheid, p. 98.

The negative language appears to take with the left hand what is given with the right. But that is no problem for the writer and all who follow in his footsteps because of their rational confidence in the mind's capacity to ascend whence being has descended:

> So there is nothing absurd in rising up, as we do, from obscure images to the single Cause of everything, rising with eyes that see beyond the cosmos to contemplate all things, even the things that are opposites, in a simple unity within the universal Cause.[21]

That might be a harmless philosophical conceit were it not for the fact that it appears to have, as a matter of historical fact, excluded other things, more important things, indeed, that need to be said about the God of Abraham, Isaac and Jacob, of the Father of our Lord Jesus Christ.

In sum, the complaints about the form taken by the doctrine of the divine attributes which descends from this influential writer, to be spelled out in later chapters, are as follows. First, the knowledge of God given in the economy of creation and redemption – those things that God has done and revealed by virtue of his action in and towards the world – have been occluded in many treatments of the divine attributes. The negative theology has in effect driven out the positive, so that the God who makes himself known in scripture has been turned into one who cannot be known as he is. Second, and it is the same point from a different angle, the divine attributes have been conceived largely cosmologically; that is, in terms of timeless relations between the eternal and the temporal, to the exclusion of attributes suggested by divine action in time. The economy

---

[21] Pseudo-Dionysius, *The Divine Names*, 821B, Luibheid, p. 100.

and revelation have been placed in a straitjacket by a conception of divine being constructed a priori. Third, this has in turn given rise to a conception of the relation of God and the world which has seen them as opposed to one another rather than as realities which are positively related in their otherness. A properly trinitarian understanding of God would rather conceive him as one who is known in his otherness only through his relation; who is known first as one who affirms the creation and only then as the creator who is distinct from the creation in order that the creation may be affirmed. But that is virtually impossible on the Dionysian account, whose movement of thought is away from this world to a timeless world beyond. Fourth, this opposition of God and the world is understood in terms of the relation of the material or sensible to the intelligible or ideal, rather than in terms of creator and created. The outcome, as we shall see, is that spirit is defined as that which is non-material, rather than that by which God is positively related to the world, sensible and intelligible alike. In the next chapter, we shall review, in this light, the chief problems that meet those who would essay a doctrine of the divine attributes.

2

A Tangled Web: An Introduction to More of the Problems

I Theology and Philosophy Again

In the previous chapter the scene was set, and one of the chief problems facing those who would attempt an account of the divine attributes was presented. It is too easy to assume that we know what is 'our idea of God', so that the essentially problematic nature of what the tradition has bequeathed us is concealed. Most of the detailed problems derive from that, and the tangled web of interrelations between the Hellenic and Hebrew traditions consequent upon it. In the light, then, of the central and dominating feature of the tradition, what are the other chief questions which beset any treatment of the attributes? They are many and various, and an illustrated account will show us how complicated and important the matter is.

1. *The relation of 'philosophy' and 'theology'*; or, more accurately in the terms we learned from Robert Jenson, the relation of Greek religion and biblical faith. We have already seen that, as with much of our theology, there are in this case especially two sources for what has been developed in the history of Christian thought, classical philosophy on the one hand and the scriptures of the Old and

New Testaments on the other. As we shall see, the former
tradition – for good reasons – tends to stress the impersonal
and metaphysical attributes, the latter the personal. One
way of bringing the two into interrelation is found in
Barth's doctrine of the divine perfections, where what we
might call the more personal of the attributes serve as
frameworks for the discussion and correction of the more
abstract and metaphysical characterizations beloved of the
classical philosophical tradition. Crucial for him is that
the apparently more philosophical of the attributes are seen
in the context of, and necessarily shaped by, the perfections derived from divine action. Characteristically, in one
example he shows the damage that an excessively philosophical approach can inflict: 'it was a retrogression when
the idea of God's *aseitas* was interpreted, or rather sup-
planted, by that of *independentia* or *infinitas*, and later by
that of the unconditioned or absolute'.[1] Barth's point is
clear: the translation or progression from aseity to *independentia* may appear to make a minor move, but in fact turns
a positive (that God is fully real in and for himself) into a
negative (that God is defined in terms of his opposition to
rather than otherness from the world). This is a theme which
will recur, and it reminds us of an essential truth about
the practice of theology: that apparently minor shifts of
content in one place can have a major impact in another.
To seek 'balance' as a primary end in theology is to court
boredom, if not disaster; yet imbalance can also be cata-
strophic. Such are the difficulties of the discipline. And yet
it is clear, as was argued in the previous chapter, that what
we encounter in this topic is more than a contrast and

---

[1] Karl Barth, *Church Dogmatics*, translation edited by G.W.
Bromiley and T.F. Torrance (Edinburgh: T. & T. Clark, 1957–1975),
2/1, p. 303.

comparison of philosophy and theology, for there also takes place – and this will be abundantly illustrated in what is to come – an encounter of theologies.

But it cannot be the use of philosophical terminology in itself that is at fault. Christianity is a philosophical faith, at least in the respect that in its main streams it has never renounced the conceptual task: the task of making clear in what manner its gospel is true, and true in the same sense that other things are true – for example the concepts and formulae in which natural scientists give accounts of their discoveries. That is to say, it must seek to give an account of the way things really are. And in connection with the doctrine of the divine attributes, that involves answering enquiries about what it means for our understanding of the being of our God that he is described as a rock and a fortress and the Father of our Lord Jesus Christ. For that matter, the meanings of such words as love, freedom and spirit are not self-evident. Love takes many forms and some freedoms are not what they claim to be, while many conceptions of spirit, especially some of those fashionable today, are not necessarily those of scripture. This means that the question of the relation of theology and philosophy is not merely historical. We cannot examine what happened when the gospel encountered the Greeks, exclude improper Greek influences, and advance without more ado. Our next problem shows us why.

2. *Divine being and divine action.* This is another version of the same problem. Greeks appear to stress a theology of divine being, Hebrews of divine action. Writing of the structural problems which are intrinsic to the Christian doctrine of God, Christoph Schwöbel identifies this one in particular: 'the antinomy between the conception of the divine attributes in philosophical theology and discourse

about divine action in Christian faith'.[2] This is illustrated by a point often made by Robert Jenson, that there is a tendency to identify the divine attributes by a list of 'omni's' and negatives – omnipotent, omniscient, omnipresent, infinite, eternal and the rest – and then paste on to them conceptions of divine action, especially that central to the Bible's account of what is called the economy of creation and redemption: the temporally structured events in which God creates, upholds, redeems and will perfect the created world. Christoph Schwöbel gives a neutral account of the relation between the traditions and suggests that

> both the conception of divine action and the theory of God's metaphysical attributes are, in spite of the tensions between them, necessary elements in a comprehensive conception of the attributes of God the creator, reconciler and redeemer of the world. . . . Although they seem *prima facie* in direct contradiction, their relationship can be conceived as *complementary*, if it is understood as one of mutual qualification.[3]

What this reveals is that, whatever else the tradition is, it is not naive, and that is why the fashionable assumption that we may simply reject certain of the ancient attributes – for example impassibility – is at best patronizing to a tradition that had good reason to say the things that it did about God. In this area, no victory can be won simply by bombing the opposition out of existence. For example, suppose that we do wish to oppose the dominance of theories of being with those of action. Is what we mean by action so self-evident, in our case let alone God's?

---

[2] Christoph Schwöbel, *God: Action and Revelation* (Kampen: Kok Pharos, 1992), p. 46.
[3] Schwöbel, *God: Action and Revelation*, p. 61.

And yet that there is a serious problem is shown by one recent topic of discussion. And it is this: a breach appears to have opened up between what God is in his relations to us and what he is claimed to be in his inner and eternal being. In terms of the doctrine of the Trinity, there appears to be a difference between the economic Trinity – that God in his actions in the world does, apparently, suffer:

> the Lord saw that the wickedness of man was great upon the earth . . . And the Lord was sorry that he had made man on the earth, and it grieved him to his heart (Gen. 6.5–6)

– and the immanent Trinity – that in his inner and eternal being God remains impassible. As one attempted solution puts it, he suffers so far as we are concerned, but not in himself:

> For when thou lookest upon us, wretched as we are, we feel the effect of thy compassion, but thou dost not feel emotion. So, then, thou art compassionate, because thou savest the wretched . . . and yet thou art not compassionate, because thou art not affected by any share in our wretchedness.[4]

The nature of the general problem – and we are not here concerned with the rights and wrongs of the specific discussion of impassibility – is clear. Sometimes a metaphysic of being seems to have so predetermined the shape of the theology of the attributes that it becomes difficult, if not impossible, to attribute to God forms of action without which the gospel ceases to be the gospel.

[4] Anselm, *Proslogion*, 8.

3. *'Absolute' and 'relative' attributes.*[5] A similar problem to that concerning the relation between divine being and divine action is the relation and distinction between the so-called 'absolute' and 'relative' attributes. Traditionally, 'absolute' attributes are those which are intrinsic to God's being – for example, aseity – while relative ones are those relative to there being a world, for example, omnipotence. (Omnipotence is an example because it seems to be the case that the exercise of power presupposes there being something over which to exercise it; grace might be another.) From observation of the way things are recounted in scripture, it seems clear that its chief focus is on the characteristics of God in action and in relation to the world. The divine attributes are, that is to say, narratively identified. From the outset of the treatment in Genesis of creation, fall and their aftermath, there is a stress on God's sovereignty (in creative action), mercy, providence and love, while his holiness dominates parts of Leviticus and his redemptive justice the prophecies of the Second Isaiah, simply to take a number of instances, not entirely at random. Yet while a number of those attributes might appear to remain relative – there is, it might appear, no mercy without a creature to whom to show it – others imply, or at least seem to imply, something absolute, love and holiness for instance. Do we not want to say both that holiness is a form of action and relation to and in the world and that it is something that characterizes the being of God in himself, absolutely; that God is not only holy in his action, especially, as P.T. Forsyth famously and repeatedly insisted, on the cross of Christ, but that he is eternally the holy one? Holiness, that is to say, is both action and attribute, both relative and

---

[5] Sometimes the distinction is between immanent and relative (or quiescent) attributes.

absolute, and is, moreover, derived more from the Bible than from philosophical theology, despite Rudolf Otto. Whether the distinction between relative and absolute is of more than minor assistance in our task will remain to be seen. At present, I am chiefly reviewing the way things have been, and especially seeking to avoid making premature generalizations.

II *Further Complications*

Before we begin a detailed examination of the problems so far identified, centring as they do on the relation between the metaphysical and the personal, being and action, the Greek and the Hebrew, it must be made clear that we have but begun to clarify the situation. There are a number of further complications which must first be reckoned with before any genuine progress can be made. We then have to take account also of the following:

4. *Difficult cases.* Some of the traditional attributes fall clearly into neither of the categories which have been distinguished – neither the 'biblical-personal' nor the 'philosophical-metaphysical' – and either appear to belong to both, or are assumed to belong to a class other than that to which they actually do belong. An example of the latter class is omnipotence, which we shall meet again and again. On the face if it, this appears to be an essentially metaphysical attribute, for it figures in the list of words beginning with 'omni-' or 'all-' which appear to be metaphysical in character. Yet the first systematic development of the concept was that of Irenaeus, a theologian whose theology was oriented rather to scripture than to philosophy, and he achieved it on biblical grounds. No Greek philosopher

would attribute omnipotence to God, for all held that at least some aspects of the world were eternal, and therefore represented an eternal limit on what God – at least, any god conceived to be in some way distinct from the world – could both be and do.[6] Yet early in the Christian tradition it came to be one of the defining attributes of God.

Why was this so? The doctrine was a specifically theological coining, a side-effect so to speak of Irenaeus' development of the doctrine of *creatio ex nihilo*, which, as he rightly saw, implied omnipotence. Or rather, and it seems likely that the two considerations came to be advanced as part of one process of thought, it was in the light of what he saw to be the omnipotent action implied in the incarnation and resurrection of Christ that he came to affirm the omnipotence of the creator in creation, who could be limited by nothing outside himself – because there was nothing outside himself: 'He who contains all things, and is himself contained by no one'.[7] In this context, omnipotence is clearly more personal than metaphysical in meaning, for it is a feature of personal agency. Scripture, we might say,

[6] That holds, as we shall see, for any position, like Plato's, which assumes a measure of distinction between God and the world. In a pantheistic system, it might be arguable that the whole universe is, in a sense, omnipotent; though even there, in view of the deterministic tendency of pantheism, it would prove difficult.

[7] Irenaeus, *Haer.*, 4. 20. 2. Although 'contain' is the usual translation for this passage (πάντα χώρων, μόνος δε ἀχώρητος ὤν), Irenaeus' theology as a whole suggests that 'enclose' might be a better translation. 'Irenaeus can speak of God "enclosing" his creation and yet only be *mis*interpreted as a pantheist. In both the cosmic and christological case there is a distinct ontological divide functioning that only avoids collapse into monism by virtue of the fact that God himself prevents such a collapse through the mediating activity of the Son and Spirit. By mediating his own being with that of his creation through his "two hands", God creates an ontological space in which duality does not collapse into dualism.' Paul Cumin, 'Irenaeus, Gnostic Monism and the Strong Second Hand of God', unpublished paper.

opens with a display of divine sovereignty which looks to be the basis of later, more systematic accounts of omnipotence. Commenting on Genesis 18.14, 'Is anything too difficult for the Lord?', Gordon Wenham observes: 'God, this passage teaches, is both omniscient and omnipotent. . . . [T]hese beliefs inform the whole of biblical narrative, but rarely are they quite so explicit as here.'[8] There is our complication in a nutshell. Being or action? Metaphysical or personal? Is there necessarily a choice? The answer is, not in this case, but others are not so clear. In this game, nothing is as straightforward as it seems.

5. Ousia *and* hypostasis. Even if we thought that we could easily come to a satisfactory account of the relation between attribute and action, or God in himself and God in his activities *ad extra* – and that way of putting it will already have alerted perceptive readers to what is coming – there is a further complication within that very distinction. The expression, 'God in himself', has two focuses. There is first of all God's eternal being as the one God; and second, his eternal being as that same God in three hypostases or persons. Clearly, there are some things which have to be said of one, some of the other; or rather, the particular persons, Father, Son and Spirit, must each have their own attributes, their own distinctive characteristics, or they would be indistinguishable from one another, and so theologically perform no function. If the persons are functionally indistinguishable – that is, indistinguishable in their modes of action – there seems little point in the doctrine of the Trinity. In much of the tradition, and for good – though possibly not sufficient – reasons, the distinction of attributes has been reduced to a minimum: 'through the Father,

[8] Gordon Wenham, *Genesis 16–50* (Dallas, Texas: Word Books, 1994), p. 49.

that is, because of the Father having the qualities, the Son and the Spirit have all their qualities, those of being unbegotten, and of birth and procession, being excepted'.[9] That is to say, the only distinction of attribute between Father, Son and Spirit is that the latter two are, respectively, begotten and proceeding.[10] Whether more should be said will be one of the central questions we must ask, for we here light upon a problem that will be with us to the end. It is indeed the case that many people in the West especially have come to believe that the doctrine of the Trinity is at best a defensive rather than a positively useful doctrine, and others that it is to be rejected altogether, so that part of the point of this book will be to suggest that, on the contrary, the doctrine of the Trinity is the key to an adequate account of the divine attributes. At this stage, however, we are chiefly listing the problems. Can one distinguish between God's attributes and the distinctive characteristics of Father, Son and Holy Spirit? The question is closely related to another.

6. *What counts as an attribute?* The matter of the distinction between the attributes of the one God and those of the three hypostases in turn raises the question of what we mean by an attribute. Are intellect and will attributes? It seems so, because the will is something a personal being appears to possess. However, to suppose such – to, so to speak, hypostatize will as a kind of distinct entity *within* a person – has been the cause of insuperable theological difficulties in understanding the relation between the doctrine

[9] John of Damascus, *De Fide Orth.*, 1. 8.
[10] Citing Gregory of Nyssa, *Against Eunomius*, 1. 22, James P. Mackey claims that according to this, 'the distinguishing properties of the Holy Spirit are described in terms which are either wholly negative or remarkably uninformative'. *The Christian Experience of God as Trinity* (London: SCM Press, 1983), p. 145.

of the Trinity and christology. If will is an attribute, it is clear that God can have only one: the idea of three divine wills is problematic for all kinds of reasons. And yet the gospel account appears to require at least two wills somewhere, as crucially in Gethsemane. When Jesus says, 'not my will, but yours be done', the gospel appears to imply that it is at least conceivable that the Son will will other than his Father. To avoid the problem of there being two wills in God, two were attributed to Christ. There must be in Christ himself, it was argued, two wills, a divine will and a human will, and what we see in Gethsemane is the human nature's will accepting that of the divine nature.

But that simply will not do. There are two reasons. First, the decision which was taken to the effect that will is an attribute of nature and not of the hypostasis or person leads to saying that natures have wills, with an inevitably Nestorian outcome. A human nature and a divine nature cannot will anything. Only persons have wills, especially if by 'will' we mean that which initiates or brings about action directed to an object or end. But if we examine what is entailed, we shall realize that it is a mistake to make will into a kind of entity or object. It means, rather, a person willing something rather than some hypostatized entity within the person of such a kind that one person can have two of them. It can be argued, second, that this position is supported by scripture. What we read in the gospel accounts of Gethsemane is an interaction between the will of the incarnate Christ – the eternal Son become man – and the will of the Father. A literal translation of Mark 14.36 is: 'not what I will but what you [will]'. Jesus is praying in the Spirit to his Father. It follows that attributes are revealed in action, because they characterize action first of all. Our salvation is achieved because here, as in the temptation in the wilderness, the incarnate Son resists the temptation to do otherwise *by willing what the Father wills*, albeit, and this is important, by the enabling power of his Father's Spirit. There appear to be at least two wills in action here and a third if it is not too fanciful to speak of the Spirit's willing Jesus' act. It perhaps is, but underlying all this is the point which must be made: that will is not an attribute but a description of a personal agent engaging in a certain form of action.

Immediately our problem looks different. We have three forms of action, albeit action in communion: the Father's action in salvation is mediated by the Son and the Spirit who are like him fully divine agents. Thus is it beautifully expressed by Edward Irving:

> My Christ is the Trinity manifested; . . . I have the Father manifest in everything which He doth; for He did not His own will, but the will of His Father. I have the Son mani-fested, in uniting His Divinity to a humanity prepared for Him by the Father; and in making the two most contrary things to meet and kiss each other . . . I have the Holy Spirit manifested in subduing, restraining, conquering, the evil propensities of the fallen manhood, and making it an apt organ for expressing the will of the Father . . . [11]

If therefore we think of the will as something characterizing the action of a person rather than being the single attribute of the one God, the problems at least look rather different. It may be that confusion has been caused by different conceptions of will. Undoubtedly, God has only one will: as the one God he wills one thing, the perfection of his

[11] Edward Irving, *The Collected Writings of Edward Irving in Five Volumes*, edited by G. Carlyle (London: Alexander Strachan, 1865), vol. 5, p. 170.

creation. This is will as *intention* rather than attribute. But
he achieves this end by the mediation of the Son and Spirit,
three wills in utterly concerted action; will as person in
action, rather than attribute.

7. *The relation between attributes.* The reference to the
Trinity immediately introduces another topic: the relation
of the attributes to one another. If there is more than one
attribute, might they not endanger the unity, or, more
classically, the simplicity of God? Indeed, are they all
compossible, consistent with one another? It is often, for
example, charged that, in the light of 'the problem of evil',
God cannot be both all good and all powerful; or in the
light of the doctrine of divine omniscience that God cannot
both know all and leave room for human freedom. The
doctrine of divine simplicity, which holds that God is
'simple uncompounded being, without diverse members
...',[12] might appear to endanger the doctrine of the Trinity,
though in itself it does not necessarily deny plurality.
Speaking of God's unity, Barth claims that 'the very unity
of [God's] being consists in the multiplicity, individuality
and diversity of His perfections . . .'[13] There have been a
number of different ways of facing this question, mostly
without reference to the Trinity. What Barth calls the
nominalist approach supposes that because the attributes
are mere attributes – qualities attributed to God by us, but
not truly touching the being of God – they cannot endanger
divine unity. He rightly rejects such an approach.

According to this all individual and distinct statements
about the being of God have no other value than that of
purely subjective ideas and descriptions . . . to which

[12] Irenaeus, *Haer.*, 2. 13. 3.
[13] Barth, *Church Dogmatics*, 2/1, p. 332.

there is no corresponding reality in God, who is pure simplicity . . . Even main stream theology gives too much weight to this position. According to the main stream of theological tradition which holds the balance in this matter, the emphasis . . . falls less upon the negation . . . than upon the positive point that the statements concerning a multiplicity of perfections in God are statements expressing our vision of God.[14]

As we have seen, Barth is content with neither of these positions. The perfections, in all their variety and richness, all characterize the essence of God, what he truly is in the relational life of the Trinity.

Another rather different attempt is that of Spinoza, who grasps the bull by the horns. Because God is infinite, his attributes must be infinite also in both number and extent; that is to say, their multiplicity is a function of the divine infinity, which is utterly simple. This leads him to a pantheist theology, because the two attributes we can know – mind and extension – are identical, and therefore – given his other Platonist assumptions that extension belongs to the world, mind to God – God and the world are one self-identical being. More recent theologians might well consider this a pseudo-problem, for it has become fashionable to deny the doctrine of divine simplicity.[15] This will not do if we wish to hold on to a doctrine of the unity and coherence of the divine being, and so our question remains. How are the various attributes related to one another, and to their common centre in the being of God?

[14] Barth, *Church Dogmatics*, 2/1, pp. 327–8. The object of Barth's critique here is almost certainly Schleiermacher.
[15] Stephen R. Holmes, "Something Much Too Plain to Say": Towards a Defence of the Doctrine of Divine Simplicity, *Neue Zeitschrift für Systematische Theologie und Religionsphilosophie* 43 (2001), 137–54.

8. *Incommunicable and communicable attributes.* Another complication is introduced by the well-known distinction, important for the Reformed tradition, between incommunicable and communicable attributes: those, to speak crudely, God keeps to himself and those he spreads around. In some respects, this is unproblematic: God makes Israel holy, but not omnipotent. It is perhaps characteristic of the Reformed tradition that the problem should be raised by it in this particular form, for as a result of the crisis of piety that had led to the Reformation a concentration on the relation of justification and sanctification raised in acute form the problem of the divine attributes. Until then, the discussion of the divine being was concentrated on the cosmological question, the context in which the matter tended to be discussed in the Middle Ages. At stake then was the relation between Being and beings, and reverberations of the critique of the Thomist analogy by Scotus, Ockham and their successors are still to work out their impact on theology. With the Reformation the focus shifts to the realm of salvation, and therefore of holy God and sinful man, with inevitable ramifications for the doctrine of God.[16]

And yet the way the matter worked itself out often reveals a confusion between different approaches to the doctrine of the attributes. The tradition became uneasy, for both theological and philosophical reasons, though chiefly the latter, it seems to me, about ever using the same words of both God and the creature. Heppe quotes the Reformed theologian Johannes Braun:

> The most notable distinction of God's attributes is that

[16] Not that this was entirely absent before; one can see it in Anselm, though not in such a way as to bear upon the question of the communicable attributes.

by which they are distinguished into communicable and incommunicable. Strictly speaking none are communicable, since they are *proprietates* (God's very own). Still, analogically and equivocally certain ones may be called communicable, because certain traces of them are found among creatures, such as knowledge, will, goodness, justice.[17]

Holiness is undoubtedly an attribute somewhere centred on divine action; it is derived from a history of personal action, and scripture clearly regards it as being communicable; indeed, the communication of holiness is the chief end of divine action in the world. Yet it does not seem important for Braun, who has clearly reverted to an essentially cosmological – 'certain traces of them are found among creatures' – rather than narrative way of construing the attributes. And that takes us to our concluding set of difficulties, which takes us full circle to the problem of philosophy and theology with which we began.

III Being and Action

9. *Cosmological and historical*. In the citation from Braun, we meet under another form the problem of the relation between divine action and the being of the world, a universal theological problem of which that of the attributes is one aspect. The specific form in which the topic is presented by Braun reveals a problem which we shall meet in all the traditions, patristic-Orthodox, medieval Catholic and, as

[17] Heinrich Heppe, *Reformed Dogmatics, Set out and Illustrated from the Sources*, translated by G. T. Thomson (Grand Rapids, Michigan: Baker, 1950), pp. 60–1.

here, Reformation. The relation between God and the world is construed, statically, in terms of pairs of concepts timelessly understood through analogy. The choice of attributes in that passage – knowledge, will, goodness and justice – is instructive in other ways, also, and indicates what will come to be seen not merely as problems to be discussed, but structural deficiencies in the tradition. For, in the light of scripture, the obvious examples to take might appear to be holiness and love, they being the divine characteristics which Israel and the church are bidden to receive and exercise from their God as a response to his action. That they ceased to be prominent among those that were treated is a symptom of an underlying disease whose character we must examine if we are to venture an account of the doctrine of God. As we shall see, they led to a rift running through the Reformed treatment of the attributes – a rift whose character will be highly informative when we come to examine it.

At this stage, however, we are more concerned to describe aspects of the problems than to essay a major critique. No doubt criticism is already implicit in the way the questions have been formulated, and that is indeed the intention. But the point to be made in summary is this: the matter, like so many problems in theology, becomes, as soon as it is pondered, far more complicated than it first appears. In this light, then, in the next chapter we shall begin an examination of some of the problems in historical context.

3

The Predominance of the Negative

I The Unknowability of God: Introduction

It is a dogma whose truth is almost everywhere stated or assumed that the human being cannot know the essence or being of God. One consequence of this for our language is that, as they stand, our words are simply incapable of speaking of the creator. That is the truth underlying what is known as the negative theology: that God can best be characterized by thinking away the limitations inherent in words designed – or so the theory goes – to speak of created things. However, what might appear to be a proper human modesty before the divine can turn into the supreme blasphemy of denying revelation. There is a fine line between a proper humility and believing that so long as we do not say anything positive we have somehow laid hold of, or come nearer to the truth about, the divine reality. There are excellent historical reasons for the development of the negative theology, and we shall meet some of them. But a necessary battle was fought with the wrong weapons.

As is clear, bound up with our topic are questions about the nature and capacity of language. The interrelation is well noted by Gregory of Nazianzus:

> For that which may be conceived may perhaps be made clear by language . . . at any rate imperfectly. . . . But to

comprehend the whole of so great a Subject as this is quite impossible and impracticable . . . even to those who are highly exalted . . . [1]

That granted, however, there are in the tradition confusions deriving from an excessive reliance on the image of sight. The concentration in many of the treatments of this topic on the impossibility of *seeing* God is a symptom of the weakness of this way of viewing [*sic*] things, for it inverts the way in which biblical revelation presents the matter. Not that there is in scripture no reference to the notion of vision – it is used in John 1.18, in the negative form we have come to know so well ('no one has seen God') – but that, as in other realms, to centre upon this one of the senses is to muddy the waters. We must pause to examine what is meant by sight in biblical revelation.

If we look generally at biblical ways of presenting the matter, we shall meet with some surprises. The first is that it is not the being of God that gives problems, but his revelatory presence, *ad extra*. 'No one can see God and live'; we should be well advised in discussing our topic to note that this has to do with God's revelation, not his essence. '"We are doomed to die" he [Manoah] said to his wife. "We have seen God"' (Judg. 13.21f.). This means that we should invert the usual order. We do not see God, but we are given to know his essence, who and what he is. And the point – which is simply being stated here, and will be expanded in a later chapter – is this: we know the being of

---

[1] Gregory of Nazianzus, *Second Theological Oration, Nicene and Post-Nicene Fathers* (Edinburgh: T. and T. Clark, 1989), vol. 7, p. 290. What this has to do with the 'exalted' we must take leave to wonder. 'I praise you, Father, Lord of heaven and earth, because you have hidden these things from the wise and learned, and revealed them to little children' (Matt. 11.25). See also 1 Cor. 1–2.

God because we are shown that God, to his very heart, is holy love. This does not mean that we see with a kind of direct vision into the inner workings of the divine. We know them, though we do not see into them. But that is a form of knowledge of God's essence. It is a kind of knowledge not by seeing but by personal relation, whose reality is the burden of the ecclesiology both of Paul and of the writer of the Gospel of John. Although we cannot know God's naked – unmediated – self-presentation, we can know him by knowing the Son, as the Fourth Gospel repeatedly insists. And we know the Son because the Father sends the Spirit in order that we should be able to do so. And those who know the Son know the Father. As John Zizioulas has taught us, life in the church is life in *koinonia*: in communion with God through its worship and life. That is a form of knowing, knowledge by acquaintance.

Calvin similarly speaks frequently of union with Christ, a being in relation to Christ which is at the same time a being in relation with God the Father.

In view therefore of scripture's confidence about the knowledge of God given by the Spirit, we shall look upon all negative theology with suspicion if it does not have a basis in some kind of positive trinitarian theology of this kind. And there is another good reason to be cautious: in its historical and intellectual origins the negative theology derives from certain forms of Greek theology, which, we might say, had good reasons for their modesty. Let us examine some of the things it had to say, or rather to deny.

II *The Negation of the Finite. The Greek Critique of their Gods*

A glance at aspects of the history of the topic will make it clear that although it is the classical contribution to the synthesis of philosophy and theology which is at the heart of our problems, a solution is not to be found by simply contrasting an impersonal Greek deity with the personal God of scripture. There is, indeed, a pressure on Greece to the impersonal, because Greek philosophical discussion of deity begins with an attack on the theology of the educators of Greece, Homer and Hesiod. The crudely anthropomorphic nature of that tradition offended the fastidious rationalism of the philosophers, just as some biblical presentations of divine action presented – and present – problems for philosophically educated Christians. Some well-known fragments of Xenophanes, from the sixth century BC, will introduce the critique which developed, a critique which is both moral and more generally philosophical:

> Homer and Hesiod have attributed to the gods everything that is a shame and reproach among men, stealing and committing adultery and deceiving each other.[2]

To the charge of anthropomorphism is added one of projection:

> The Ethiopians say that their gods are snub-nosed and black, the Thracians that theirs have light blue eyes and red hair.[3]

---

[2] Xenophanes, Fragment 11, G. S. Kirk and J. E. Raven, *The Presocratic Philosophers. A Critical History with a Selection of Texts* (Cambridge: Cambridge University Press, 1957), p. 168.

[3] Xenophanes, Fragment 16, Kirk and Raven, *The Presocratic Philosophers*, p. 168.

According to Eric Osborn, Xenophanes' contribution to a
solution was to conceive God as universal mind. 'Equally
daring is the claim that this one intellectual god directly and
drastically affects the physical world; "without toil he
makes all things by the thought of his mind".'[4] This notion
of God as essentially intellect has one of its logical and
historical outcomes in Aristotle's doctrine of God in the
Nicomachean Ethics, that God is to be conceived as thought
contemplating itself.[5] Denying most forms of activity to
God, yet conceding life to him, Aristotle argues that 'if
action is taken away from a living being . . . what remains
but contemplation (θεωρία)?'[6] But that is the problem
rather than the solution. To conceive God primarily in
terms of intellect, with priority given to contemplation
rather than action, renders the conception antithetical to a
concept of God whose being is known primarily through
his historical and particular action. This is not to suggest
that the biblical God lacks intellect, but rather that his
intellectuality is understood in terms of wisdom: that is to
say, practical intellect, intellect *directed to* rather than
abstracted from involvement in created being. Speaking of
God's wisdom, Proverbs 8 affirms: 'The Lord brought me
forth as the first of his works . . . I was there when he set the
heavens in place' (Prov. 8.22, 27). That is also the case with
Irenaeus, who always celebrates God's intellect in connection with his doctrine of creation. At the heart of the Bible's
account of God is an orientation to action, not contempla-

---

[4] Eric Osborn, *Irenaeus of Lyons* (Cambridge: Cambridge University
Press, 2001), p. 34.
[5] And perhaps the Epicurean gods, existing in bliss with no interest in
the world, are thus not finally so different.
[6] Aristotle, *Ethics* 1178b20–21. Notice once again the centrality of
sight.

tion, and this must determine the way in which we consider his being and attributes.

Of Xenophanes Edward Caird comments rather more appropriately that, 'We have here a criticism of the human-ised Polytheism of Greece, a criticism which rests on the basis of an abstract Pantheism and repudiates the idea of giving any form whatsoever to the absolute being, even the form of man himself. In other words, we have here the idea of God as the mere negation of the finite.'[7] It is worth noting that in his attempt to give an account of the principle (*arche*) of things, Anaximander had described it as the *apeiron*, the infinite or unbounded, describing it in terms of what it is not. That Kirk and Raven translate this as 'the indefinite' is particularly illuminating of the sheer abstraction of the concept.[8] This is a theme that will recur, repeatedly, and raises the question of what we mean when we say that God is infinite; as we shall see, there is more than one possible definition. But the tendency of Greek theology to monism or pantheism is further confirmation of the fact that we have here a real clash between theologies, not first and second stages of a neat progression.

There is more to be said about the Greek theology which has so influenced the Christian, and the difference of Plato's development from Xenophanes' moral critique shows that there are other features of the development than the merely negative. In the second book of *The Republic*, the philo-

---

[7] Edward Caird, *The Evolution of Theology in the Greek Philosophers* (Glasgow: James MacLehose and Sons, 1904), vol. 1, p. 62. We recall here Ezek. 1.26. At the heart of the vision of God, 'and seated above the likeness of a throne was a likeness as it were of a human form'. Once again, Irenaeus, who appealed to this text, knew better what was at stake than many of his apparently more sophisticated successors. Irenaeus, *Haer.*, 4. 20. 10–11.

[8] Kirk and Raven, *The Presocratic Philosophers*, p. 104.

sopher's discontent with the demoralizing effect of the stories of the gods serves as the basis for a renewed and positive account of the divine attributes. First, argues Plato, God is truly good, and must be described only as such, which means, we should note, that he is not omnipotent, for life brings more evil than good, so that the former must be attributed to another source than God: 'God is not the author of all things, but of the good alone.'[9] Second, God is 'simple, and of all things abides steadfast in his own form'.[10] This follows from the fact that, as a perfect being, God cannot suffer change from without; indeed, because any change from what is perfect can only be for the worse, there can be no change in God at all. The chief implication of this is that God does not lie, particularly by taking up lying forms in order to deceive. 'God is entirely simple and true in both act and word, and neither changes himself nor deludes others, either in images or word, or by sending signs. . . .'[11]

Plato's outline account of three divine attributes – goodness, impassibility and simplicity – is scarcely designed to serve as a theology, being mainly devised as a means of purifying the educational literature of which he was providing a critique. In later centuries, however, the philosophies labelled variously as Platonic represented in part an attempt to develop a more systematic theology, and formed, along with their rivals, the penumbra within which the first Christian theologians did their thinking. In so far as it came to a kind of climax in the thought of Plotinus, this tradition represented essentially a development of Xenophanes' and Parmenides' negative theology. Let us see what Plotinus

---

[9] Plato, *Republic*, 379–80.
[10] Plato, *Republic*, 380.
[11] Plato, *Republic*, 382e8–11.

made of the divine attributes, and move on to trace some of the echoes of the tradition of which he is so important an example in Christian thought.

Plotinus' chief aim is as fully as possible to deprive the concept of God of any definite characteristics. That he speaks of the One rather than of God need not trouble us, for the object of our quest is the language in which the lineaments of the being of the supposed source of all are sketched. According to Rist's account, the One is 'without form . . . or a shapeless form . . .; strictly speaking it is indescribable . . . no name can be appropriate to it . . . It is simply "the not this".[12] The chief point to note is that any positive characterization is a mistake. According to Copleston:

> God is absolutely transcendent: He is the One, beyond all thought and all being, ineffable and incomprehensible . . . Neither essence nor being nor life can be predicated of the One, [and here we reach the inevitable escape clause] not of course that it is less than any of these things, but because it is *more*, τὸ ὑπὲρ πάντα ταῦτα εἶναι.[13]

The key point is perhaps this:

> Since God is one, without any multiplicity or division, there can be in the One no duality of substance and accident, and Plotinus is accordingly unwilling to ascribe to God any positive attributes . . . Nevertheless, goodness may be ascribed to the One, provided that it is *not*

---

[12] J. M. Rist, *Plotinus: The Road to Reality* (Cambridge: Cambridge University Press, 1967), p. 25.

[13] Frederick Copleston, *A History of Philosophy*, volume 1, *Greece and Rome* (Westminster, Maryland: The Newman Press, 1966), p. 464.

attributed to an inhering quality. . . . . Moreover, we can legitimately ascribe to the One neither thought nor will nor activity.[14]

Plotinus is not, of course, a Christian theologian, and those theologians who drew on him had necessarily to qualify what they borrowed. Yet the borrowing – and here Plotinus, for all his refinement of earlier philosophy, is representative of the heart of a tradition stretching back to Anaximander – had, and continues to have, far too deep an influence on theology. Notice one uncomfortable implication of such a teaching: we cannot, if we take this to be a universal rule, attribute even goodness and love to God as an inhering, inner quality. Do we find such claims made in Christian writers?

III The Unknowability of God. Aspects of the Early Christian Tradition.

Parts of the early Christian tradition show signs of being excessively dominated by a stress on the negative attributes of God and the negative way to know and describe him. Origen is a case in point and his opening account of God the Father begins with a discussion of what it means to say that God is spirit mainly in terms of its (for him by no means unambiguous) implications of bodilessness. Here is the beginning of a tendency which is met again and again, that 'spirit' means that which is non-material. Origen denies that 'we should attribute to God any material characteristics, we assert that in truth he is incomprehensible and immeasurable'. He continues:[15]

[14] Copleston, *A History of Philosophy*, vol. 1, p. 465, italics added.
[15] Origen, *Princ.*, 1. 1. 5.

God therefore must not be thought to be any kind of body ... but to be a simple intellectual existence, admitting in himself of no addition whatever, so that he cannot be believed to have in himself a more or less, but is a Unity, or if I may so say, Oneness throughout, and the mind and fount from which originates all intellectual existence and mind.[16]

Notice the dominating features: the denial of bodiliness and an affirmation of pure intellectuality. Moving on to a brief discussion of God's intrinsic invisibility, Origen concludes the first chapter of his work – before moving on to the person of Christ – with the claim that he has now 'investigated the nature of God'.[17] Absent, we must notice, is any treatment of attributes drawn from the economy. Let me repeat: God is defined without reference either to narrative or to anything trinitarian. Whatever Origen wants also to say later, we are at this crucial and determinative stage restricted to an essentially philosophically and intellectually conceived deity.

Other accounts of attributes conceived essentially negatively are plentiful in the early tradition. The opening sections of John of Damascus' *De Fide Orthodoxa* are here remarkable, if depressing. The tradition has been Christianized, to be sure, yet it is still part of the same tradition, as some of the forms of argument will suggest. The pattern can be discerned in the very first chapter of the book. God is 'ineffable and incomprehensible' although a limited knowledge is given in revelation – 'that which it was to our profit to know'. The attributes with which John begins – and so shapes everything that follows – share common features with Plato's discussion:

[16] Origen, *Princ.*, I. I. 6. Why does God originate only 'intellectual existence and mind'?

[17] Origen, *Princ.*, I. I. 9.

God, being good, is the cause of all good, subject neither to envy nor to any passion. For envy is far removed from the divine nature, which is both passionless and only good.

And then, in chapter 2, comes something like a systematic account. Notice particularly how the negatives are piled up before a list of more positive characteristics is appended:

God is without beginning, without end, eternal and everlasting, uncreate, unchangeable, invariable, simple, uncompound, incorporeal, invisible, impalpable, uncircumscribed, infinite, incognisable, indefinable, incomprehensible, good, just, maker of all things created, almighty, all-ruling, all-surveying, of all overseer, sovereign, judge; and that God is One, . . . and [rather as an afterthought, it must be said] has his being in three hypostases.

The negatives are piled one upon another before anything else is said. Then, reminded by the allusion to the Trinity, John launches into a summary of the Niceno-Constantinopolitan creed, before returning to abstract discussion. The crucial 'give-away' remark comes in the fourth chapter of the first book. 'For when you speak of him as good, and just, and wise, and so forth, you do not tell God's nature but only the qualities of his nature.' Note the echo of the theology of Plotinus as it appears in Copleston's account: 'goodness may be ascribed to the One, provided that it is not attributed to an inhering quality. . . .' That, it seems to me, is simply wrong.[18]

---

[18] We must not fail to mention that, when doing christology, John effectively contradicts himself, like so many of his successors who are too good theologians to be content with servitude to the Greeks. John of Damascus, *On the Divine Images* 1. 2: 'It is disastrous to suppose that the Church does not know God as He really is . . .' See also 1. 4: 'I boldly draw an image of the invisible God, not as invisible, but as having become visible for our sakes . . .'

Why it is wrong has already been suggested at the end of the previous chapter and affirmed at the beginning of this one; it will also be the subject of later chapters. The gospel assures us that we know God as he truly is. We must be content here to ask why John takes the path that he does. The problem is twofold. On the one hand he is dominated by cosmological considerations and, despite citing the creed, is in the main not interested in considerations taken not from divine action in time, but from temporality in general. But that masks a confusion. It is one thing to say that our words must be purged of references to created things, though, in view of the incarnation, even that is highly doubtful; it is quite another to think that this can be satisfactorily achieved by a denial of those things we happen to think are the characteristics of created reality. John gives the game away with a remark made in explanation of what he is doing. 'For things which are opposed in the nature of their existence must also be opposed in the mode of their existence, that is to say, must have opposite properties . . .'[19] But that is precisely the problem with which we are concerned, for it contains an implicit denial of the goodness of the creation. One is tempted to indulge in flights of Barthian rhetoric. God and the world *opposed* realities? Here we come to the heart of the problem, for an adequate doctrine of creation will affirm that the creator makes a world that is other than he, but not opposed to him – apart from sin, that is. The negative theology runs the risk, if not more, of identifying existence with fallenness. If we are to understand what is at stake, an important distinction must therefore be drawn. By created things is often meant in this – Platonic – tradition material things. But that is to assume

[19] John of Damascus, *De Fide Orth.*, 1. 3.

that createdness and materiality are equivalent and, apparently, that what we call mind or spirit is uncreated, a completely false assumption. There is simply too much evidence in the tradition for this tendency to be denied: God is defined as pure Spirit, by which is meant non-materiality. But is that what is meant when we say that God is Spirit? We shall return to the question in later chapters.

On the other hand, John of Damascus uses scripture woodenly, and he seems to operate by proof-text rather than by attempting to look at the broad picture. For example, the basis of this particular treatment is an admittedly central text in the Fourth Gospel: 'No one has ever seen God; God's only Son ... has made him known' (John 1.18). John uses this text as a peg on which to hang what is in part a repetition – albeit with additions; this is not a straightforward matter – of the main lines of the development we have traced from the Presocratics to Plotinus. The outcome is a relatively abstract account of God's attributes, stressing not the implications of the Word made flesh, as is the weight of the Fourth Gospel's account, but 'no one has seen God'. By John of Damascus' time, things had settled into a pattern: the Greek critique of the Homeric gods had come to dominate the treatment of the doctrine of God in Christian theology without at this crucial stage being corrected by considerations taken from the second half of the proof-text, that God's only Son has made him known. It had come to be believed that one can find God by negating the supposed characteristics of the ordinary structures of reality as we perceive them, something which is achieved by negating the 'material' meaning of the words. It is a kind of Platonism which assumes that any reference to matter will necessarily be inimical to an account of the attributes, any purely intellectual account somehow nearer to the truth. In this context, ontological assumptions – about the superiority of the intellectual realm to the material – and assumptions about language go hand in hand. Language purified of any material reference is somehow nearer to God, rather strangely when the teaching comes from the pen of one who cites a text claiming that God's only (incarnate) Son has made him known. But then, Jesus, the Word made material, seems to have fallen out of the picture.[20]

IV *The Unknowability of God. Aspects of the Later Christian Tradition*

It is fashionable to claim that the account of God's being and attributes in the Prima Pars of Aquinas' *Summa Theologiae* is not rightly described as a natural theology. It undoubtedly is not, if by natural theology is meant a theological enterprise carried on in complete abstraction from the Christian faith. A work, however, is to be judged not by what it sets out to do but by what it achieves, and there is more than a little evidence for the fact that Aquinas' treatment is shaped by the depressing syndrome that we have met so far. Two features of the work will support the argument. The first is centred on a much-quoted statement of principle which indicates that Aquinas belongs in the

---

[20] What is said in this topic often seems to smack more of the *logos asarkos* than of the incarnate Christ. That is wrong, at least if we take our orientation from the crucial biblical text for the whole of the argument of this book, 1 John 4.7: 'he who loves . . . knows God'; v. 9: 'This is how God showed his love among us: He sent his one and only Son into the world that we might live through him'; v. 16: 'we know and believe. . . . God is love'. There are two features to be noted. First, this is knowledge by relation: that a form of relation to God is created 'vertically' by the movement of God into the world, and this takes shape in transformed personal relations. But, second, it gives rise to a form of knowledge *that*: a knowledge of the being of God as love.

tradition which so marked the opening chapters of John of Damascus' work:

> Now we cannot know what God is, but only what He is not; we must therefore consider ways in which God does not exist, rather than ways in which he He does. We treat then first, of the ways in which God does not exist, secondly of the ways in which we know Him, thirdly of the ways in which we describe Him.[21]

This appears to imply that negative attributes are really more true of the being of God than those described as positive, and that that is indeed the case is demonstrated by Aquinas' theory of analogical predication. According to this, our attempted positive characterizations of God apply not so much to God's being, as to our way of describing God's being.[22] As the later discussion shows, this is by no means all that Aquinas says, nor is it right to say that he denies that positive characteristics can be predicated of God. Indeed, he sometimes even appears to privilege the positive names. While 'negative names applied to God . . . do not at all signify his His substance, but rather express the distance of the creature from Him', there is something apparently more favourable to be said of the positive, that, 'these names signify the divine substance . . . although they fall short of a full representation of Him'. With that, many would agree. The problem is that Aquinas appears to present us with false alternatives: 'We cannot know the essence of God in this life, as He really is in Himself; but we

---

[21] Aquinas, *Summa Theologiae*, 1a. 2, Conclusion.
[22] Schleiermacher has to take only a short step to say that 'neither in isolation nor taken together do the attributes express the Being of God in itself . . .', F. D. E. Schleiermacher, *The Christian Faith*, translated by H. R. Mackintosh and J. S. Stewart (Edinburgh: T. & T. Clark, 1928), p. 198.

know Him accordingly as He is presented to us in the perfections of creatures; and thus the names imposed by
us [*sic*] signify Him in this manner only.'[23] Once again,
construal is restricted to cosmology. Where, we must ask,
are the economy of creation and salvation and the Trinity?[24]
Might not both suggest, indeed, demand, a rather different
approach?

When we come to the second feature, Aquinas' treatment
of the content of the doctrine of the attributes, the case is
reinforced, for the fact is that the negative, metaphysical
and impersonal attributes so dominate the discussion that
the personal and action-based attributes appear to have
been marginalized. The attributes placed at the head of the
discussion are strongly metaphysical and scarcely personal
in content. Among them are simplicity, unchangeableness
and oneness, all of which may indeed have their place, but
there is nothing of mercy and justice until much else has
been discussed: until the cosmological framework has been
supplied not by a doctrine of personal triune creation but
by a process of causal abstraction. At the very least the
metaphysical precedes the personal in the order of treatment, and the absence of an early appearance of the love of
God suggests the worst. Indeed, the (very brief, and indeed
odd) discussion of the love of God appears only at Question
20, and there is no treatment at all of holiness.

Evidence that the formulation owes more to natural
theology than to revelation is provided by the way in which

---

[23] Aquinas, *Summa Theologiae*, 1a. 13. 2, ad 3.
[24] We have already seen the reason for their absence. They have been
displaced by a combination of the three famous ways owed ultimately to
Proclus and Plotinus: the negative way, the positive way and the way of
causality, all of them abstracting cosmological patterns in order to arrive
at a structured account of the divine attributes before God's particular,
incarnational interaction with the created world is mentioned.

concepts are derived. For example, the discussion of divine
simplicity is almost entirely based on a priori considerations, beginning with the denial of bodiliness to God, while
that of God's goodness is based on a prior analysis of the
general notion of goodness. The account of God's love is in
no way indebted to a theology of the Trinity, the only faintly
trinitarian reference being to whether or not God loves
Christ more than he loves everything else. Similarly, the
treatment of omnipotence notoriously defines it, again in a
priori terms, as the capacity to do everything but will
a contradiction, there being no reference to what God
actually does in the economy of creation and redemption.
That is to say, Aquinas having set up the ontological framework for his theology in the Five Ways by means of a
general philosophical analysis of causation, everything else
follows by a process of logical deduction. The attributes are
those appropriate to a being who is the moving, efficient,
material, formal and final cause of the cosmos. We have an
analysis of the God–world relation in largely cosmological
terms, untrammelled by reference to those particular divine
acts in which God is revealed by scripture actually to
operate. That is to say, the basic concepts come from philosophical, or, should we say, Greek theology. We are in the
presence of an entrenched tradition which owes more to
Greece than scripture and, despite modification, dominates
the treatment of the attributes until this day.[25]

[25] Its persistence is indicated by a strange reappearance in an
apparently odd place of the way of eminence. Immanuel Kant's first two
critiques are devoted to, among other things, the denial of the knowability of God. And yet in a footnote in the second of them, Kant appears to
be quite confident of the content of 'our idea of God': 'God has certain
properties attributed to him which, as regards the quality exhibited by
them, we find to be applicable also to created beings, the sole difference
being that, in his case, they are raised to the highest possible degree. For
example, there are these: might, knowledge, being present, kindness,

In certain important respects, there is but a hair's breadth between Aquinas and Kant. To put it another way: push the negative method but a little way in an agnostic direction, and agnosticism is the outcome. In certain essential respects, Kant's theology is but that of Aquinas radicalized. Kant is the fate of the negative theology transposed into a mechanistic world. Allow the treatment of the doctrine of God to be dominated by cosmology, and a change in cosmology will threaten the doctrine. That is to say, move from a world which is understood, with the help of Plato and his successors, to be an upwardly straining and pointing ontological hierarchy, to one understood essentially mechanistically, and the revised concept of transcendence excludes God from the world. To be sure, that is not necessarily a problem. Christian faith does not live by being conformable to the ideologies of the day. But there are two persistent theological weaknesses which are intrinsic to the development. The first is that in rightly denying that human characteristics can simply be ascribed to God, the tradition allowed itself to be determined by its negative method. Instead of defining God from revelation, it defined him as that which the world is not. There is a distinction, which is far more than the metaphorical hair's breadth, between

etc. And the designations which we employ in connection with these are: infinite might, omniscience, omnipresence, infinite kindness, etc.' Immanuel Kant, *Critique of Practical Reason*, translated by Ernst Cassirer (Milwaukee: Marquette University Press, 1998), p. 165. Highly paradoxical about all this is that Kant's essentially negative methodology has, when it comes to moral philosophy, led him to an account of the attributes owing far more to the way of eminence, the attributing to God of human powers magnified, than to the negative tradition which we meet for the most part unchanged in many theologians from Xenophanes to the present day. But then the inadequacy of the method necessarily induces a tendency to swing from one extreme to another, as we have seen in the fact that the negative theology also gives rise to a tendency to occlude the distinction between God and man.

asserting the distinction between creator and creation and developing on the basis of the negative relation a constructive theological teaching. This can even be charged of some of the things that Irenaeus said in the heat of his justified campaign to refute gnostic anthropomorphism, and of aspects of the thought of the Cappadocians, who in their desire to reject the rationalist confidence of Eunomius that God could be known overplayed the card. And the reason they overplayed it takes us to the second weakness, which is their reliance on dualistic and heavily intellectual categories to contrast the creator with the created. As we shall see, to say that God is spirit is not equivalent to saying that he is not matter. To stress that God is pure intellect runs the risk of privileging the intellectual over the material in such a way that the knowledge of God mediated through Israel's history and the incarnation – those material forms of being – becomes irrelevant to a doctrine of God's attributes.

4

From Scripture to Scotus

I *The Biblical Critique of Anthropomorphism*

It is not only the Greek philosophers who have produced critiques of the anthropomorphic pagan deities. There is a biblical equivalent, and it is very different from the tradition of cosmologically grounded philosophical theology. In sharp contrast to the latter, it proceeds by assertion, not negation. Two examples will indicate the difference. The first is the critique in the book of Genesis of the gods of the culture surrounding Israel. Implicit in the way in which its author presents what can only be called its demythologized version of the ancient myths is a theology of the divine attributes which overturns the rival theologies. Genesis 1 presents a revelation of the powerlessness of the pagan deities. Over against claims that the sun and the moon are gods, our author simply asserts that they are placed where they are by an act of divine sovereignty. We cannot say it too often: Genesis presents an account of the knowledge of God the creator, not by negation but by affirmation of his power and absolute creativity, incomparable with anything attributed to the pagan gods. It is noteworthy that in Genesis 1.14–17 the reason for the creation of the heavenly lights is given before their creation is described. Why such an apparently illogical order of treatment? It is most likely

to prevent them from being considered divinities. 'In neigh-
bouring cultures, the sun and the moon were some of the
most important gods in the pantheon, and the stars were
often credited with controlling human destiny.'[1] This is
absolutely ruled out by our passage. God may allow the
lights to 'rule over the day and over the night', but only as
his creatures. It should be noted in how matter-of-fact a
manner this is stated, simply continuing as it does a
theology of creation as a realm in which life can take place:
the lights are there to divide the day from the night; to mark
the seasons, days, years; and to give light on the earth. This
is emphasized in verse 15: 'let them [the lights] be for lights'
– that is, for nothing else, and certainly not to be wor-
shipped. It is, however, the next verse which above all distinguishes Genesis absolutely from all other versions of the
creation myth, with its wonderful throwaway line: 'and he
made the stars also'. This author simply devotes a brief
clause to what other cultures regarded as gods.[2]

The Noah story introduces us to another attribute.
Despite all apparent indications to the contrary, it is at
once a narrative account of God's immutability and a
moral critique of the pagan gods. On the face of it, God is
presented as rather changeable, in repenting and changing
his mind, and although we would be right not to take this
literally – whatever that might mean – it does not follow
that it should be entirely philosophized in the way that has

[1] Gordon Wenham, *Genesis 1–15* (Dallas, Texas: Word Books,
1987), p. 21.
[2] There is plentiful other evidence also. 'God created the great
creatures of the sea . . .' (verse 21) These are not, as in the myths of the
pagans, divine bodies from which the earth was created, but simply
God's creatures. A similar point can be made about the divine rest on the
seventh day. Far from being a limitation on God – as if he was tired,
which is not suggested – this reinforces the freedom and sovereignty with
which this book describes God's work.

sometimes happened. In his account of the divine constancy Barth prefaces his discussion of the biblical passages referring to God's repenting and apparently changing his mind with the following argument against the necessity of construing God's immutability in a Platonizing manner:

> God is constantly one and the same. But. . . His consistency is not as it were mathematical. . . . The fact that He is one and the same does not mean that He is bound to be and say and do only one and the same thing, so that all the distinctions of His being, speaking and acting are only a semblance, only the various refractions of a beam of light which are eternally the same. This was and is the way that every form of Platonism conceives God. It is impossible to overemphasise the fact that here . . . God is described as basically without life, word or act. Biblical thinking about God would rather submit to confusion with the grossest anthropomorphism than to confusion with this the primary denial of God. . . . God is certainly the immutable, but as the immutable He is the living God and He possesses a mobility and elasticity. . . [3]

Once there is a creation, and once it has fallen, it is clear that God allows himself to be affected by the antics of his creatures. But the overall point of the saga of Noah is the contrast between God's moral constancy and the ludicrous behaviour of the pagan gods. Take the parallel in the Gilgamesh epic, a polytheistic account incorporating rival gods, not all of them in favour of the plan, whose general

[3] Karl Barth, *Church Dogmatics*, translation edited by G. W. Bromiley and T. F. Torrance (Edinburgh: T. & T. Clark, 1957–1975), 2/1, p. 496.

frivolity contrasts with the moral seriousness of the Genesis account. 'According to the extrabiblical accounts, the heavenly council of the gods led by Anu and Enlil decided to destroy mankind, for multiplying too much and making too much noise.'[4] The pettiness of their motives contrasts with God's utter seriousness in this account. It is a kind of account of God's immutability, in the sense which Barth has isolated, preferring, however, to speak of God's constancy rather than immutability. 'God's constancy – which is a better word than the suspiciously negative word "immutability" – is the constancy of His knowing, willing and acting, and therefore of His person.'[5] This is indeed one of the places where Christian theology can gladly adopt aspects of Greek argument. Echoing Plato, Gregory of Nazianzus employs the doctrine of divine impassibility to absolve God from any suggestion of envy: 'And this not out of envy, for envy is far from the Divine Nature, which is passionless, and only good and Lord of all; especially of that which is the most honourable of all the creatures.'[6] The problem, as always when the doctrine of impassibility is under consideration, is whether such an argument rules out too much: not only envy, but, for example, the wrath of God against sin and evil.

Our second example is the Second Isaiah's critique of the idols. In this the theology of divine omnipotence implicit in Genesis is made definitely explicit. In the account in chapter 55 of the power of God's word to achieve what it sets out to do, we have a real link with Genesis' account of creation by word. But we find also, earlier in the chapters

---

[4] Wenham, *Genesis 1–15*, p. 164.

[5] Barth, *Church Dogmatics*, 2/1, p. 495.

[6] Gregory of Nazianzus, *Second Theological Oration*, 11. Nicene and Post-Nicene Fathers (Edinburgh: T. & T. Clark, 1989), vol. 7, p. 292.

attributed to this prophet, apparent support for the negative theology. The question is repeated: 'To whom then will you compare God? What image will you compare him with?' (Isa. 40.18) '"To whom will you compare me? Or who is my equal?", says the Holy One' (v. 25). The form of the questions might clearly expect the answer, 'Nothing', and yet the whole passage is set in the context of a revealed theology of creation in which affirmations of a wholly positive kind are made about God's power as it is manifest in creative action. The God of this writer is known through his redemptive historical action, and it is this which founds Isaiah's confidence that God is Israel's *goel*, or next of kin, the word that has come to be translated 'redeemer' and so to form the basis for a whole theology of God's holy love. This is an image, concrete and personal, with which God can indeed be compared. Drawing on the tradition of God's redemption of Israel from Egypt, the prophet compares God to the one whose responsibility it was to redeem a family member from slavery, so that his critical theology is only directed against the idols and does not provide the basis of the kind of independent negative theology which we meet in the tradition. The critique is based on affirmation; it does not, like the negative tradition, serve as the shaky foundation on which later affirmations of divine activity are often rather contradictorily constructed. We are presented with a theology of mediation rather than attribution. In that respect, we have a repetition of the point made in connection with the traditional exegesis of Exodus 3, where, as we saw in chapter 1, although the writer interprets the mysterious revelation of God narratively, the tradition generally fails to move beyond a purely philosophical and abstract notion of divine being.

II Why the 'Negative Way' is Not as Negative as it Claims

The argument has been concentrated so far on the negative theology in order to expose the nature of a programme which derives an account of the being of God by denying that God is as the material world is. As we saw from the point made by Schleiermacher in the opening chapter, however, the basis of both the negative and the apparently contrasting way of eminence is the way of causality. According to this, supposedly positive attributes of the created world are attributed to God in eminent form, by, for example, projecting infinite power from our knowledge of finite power. Corresponding to the causal structure of the world, which sees it as caused from above by the divine reality, is a movement of the mind upward from the perceived structures of the material world to the immaterial reality presiding over it. It is the way of ascent, and, according to such a cosmological conception, the world is conceived timelessly rather than historically. An example of this tendency was given in a citation in chapter 2 from the Reformed dogmatician Johannes Braun, who claimed that the universe exhibits within its structures traces of features which are analogous to the divine.

The way of causality is essentially a way of discovering the attributes of God by a process of analogy. In this case, analogy is not in the first place a method of predication – of showing how language works – but an ontological process which consists in moving from the lower levels of reality to the higher, until the whole hierarchy is argued to require as its cause – its efficient, material, formal and final cause – a being who is totally other than it. Aquinas' doctrine of analogical predication is thus grounded in what Robert

Jenson has called the ontological analysis contained in the Five Ways.[7] From this analysis, which depends upon a hierarchical structuring of reality,[8] flow many things, noteworthy among them the doctrine of the divine attributes which succeeds them rapidly in Aquinas' account. That doctrine accordingly depends, in essence, on a christianized form of Neoplatonism, whose movement from the utterly and formlessly material to the ineffably intellectual (Plotinus) is, so to speak, mirrored in the essentially similar structure of natural theology. A certain account of analogical predication is bound up with this ontology, inextricable from it. It holds that the same predicates apply to beings which exist on different levels of the hierarchy of being, but that they apply analogically, proportionally, so that they are more really true of the higher levels than the lower. Analogy, that is to say, is a theory of predication that depends upon a (Neoplatonic) theory of degrees of being, a theory most evident in Aquinas' Fourth Way, which assumes an equation of being with goodness, both of them hierarchically construed.

> Some things are found to be more good, more true, more noble, and so on, and other things less. But such comparative terms describe varying degrees of approximation to a superlative . . .[9]

---

[7] Robert W. Jenson, *The Knowledge of Things Hoped For. The Sense of Theological Discourse* (New York: Oxford University Press, 1969), ch. 3.

[8] See Anthony Kenny's account of the Aristotelian conception of movement supporting the first and crucial way, that from motion. It is hierarchical in that the movement is not traced backwards, as is often supposed – as in the picture of one domino causing another to fall in temporal series – but upwards. Thus a stick is moved by a hand, which is moved by a human soul, which is, ultimately, moved by God. *The Five Ways* (London: Routledge and Kegan Paul, 1969), ch. 2, especially pp. 24–7.

[9] Aquinas, *Summa Theologiae*, 1a. 2. 3.

It is a world-view in which the lower levels of reality mirror but dimly the divine reality which presides over them, while the higher levels – the 'spiritual' and intellectual; that is, the non-material – mirror them more brightly.

Three points must be made about this ontology and system of predication. The first is that it works by projection from below rather than by response to particular historical revelation within the structures of time and space. That is the reason why concepts of holiness and love are not really of interest to it, or, if they are, are posterior to the metaphysical concepts which set the tone and provide the foundation. In certain respects, it holds, God is utterly unlike the material world: immovable, impassible, infinite (meaning without the kind of limits we experience in the world) and eternal (meaning timeless). Given the way of causality, the method succeeds. But given a different metaphysical background, they appear to be *merely* projections, so that Feuerbach's famous objections appear to be justified. The real objection, however, is not that there is nothing to be said for versions of all of the attributes that are arrived at in this way, but that they are projected in the light of an assumed opposition between God and the world. A parallel process operates in the case of the way of eminence. Certain things are claimed to be metaphysically positive in meaning – goodness, power, and so on – and so are projected to infinity. This has a particular effect on the doctrine of divine omnipotence, tending to suggest the validation of power in general rather than the discernment of the particular power that works through the cross and of the Spirit who raised Jesus from the dead.

As we have seen, one flaw in all such theories is that they are open to the objection that they are mere projection. To be sure, that is an objection, which, other things being equal, should not be taken too seriously. Projection may reach the truth, and the question is not whether a conception has its origins in the human mind but whether it is true. Yet other things are not equal, for the whole development is over-dependent on a pagan metaphysic which militates against the possibility of saying certain things that should be said about God on the grounds of revelation, with the result that they are not said often or strongly enough and, in some cases, not at all. In place of a knowledge of God the Father mediated through his Son, we are offered intuitive or unitive knowledge of an essentially unitarianly conceived God reached by a process of unmediated ascent – unmediated, at any rate, by anything material like the human Christ; that is to say, it is a process which is begun mediately, but ultimately reaches for the immediate, and kicks away the ladder of mere material things once the summit of the hierarchy is reached.

The second point is that the apparent modesty and humility of the negative way masks quite a different movement, a movement for unity with God which operates apart from that communion mediated through Jesus which is at the heart of the Christian way. God the Son's trinitarian movement 'from above' – from eternity into time – is displaced by a cosmological movement of thought from below, out of time into the timeless realm of mystical union, with its pantheistic overtones. It is noteworthy, to take an example from a writer whose later work rightly rejected this kind of mysticism of ascension, that the 'negative way' is insidiously a way to a merging with God. It was the apophatic Barth of the *Epistle to the Romans*, who wrote that, 'The vast distinction between God and man is their veritable union.'[10] Much of what he wrote in what is

[10] Karl Barth, *The Epistle to the Romans*, translated by E. C. Hoskyns (Oxford: Oxford University Press, 1933), p. 114.

apparently a celebration of God's complete otherness could be a modernized version of Pseudo-Dionysius:

> God is known as the Unknown God. As such, He is precisely no 'thing-in-itself' [an allusion, as scarcely needs pointing, to that equally negative theologian, Immanuel Kant] . . . On the contrary, He is the eternal, pure Origin of all things. As their non-existence, He is their true being.[11]

and:

> God is pure negation. He is both 'here' and 'there'. He is the negation of negation in which the other world contradicts this world and this world the other world.[12]

The assertions of the utter otherness of God and the tendency to mystical union are two sides of the same coin, for the one so easily collapses into the other, and for good reasons, the chief one being that the otherness conceals a continuity between the human mind and the eternal which, by escaping the toils of materiality, finds itself alone with the alone. Thus Pseudo-Dionysius, distinguishing the negative from the positive way, writes of the former:

> my argument now rises from what is below up to the transcendent, and the more it climbs, the more language falters, and when it has passed up and beyond the ascent, it will turn silent completely, since it will finally be at one with him who is indescribable.[13]

[11] Barth, *The Epistle to the Romans*, pp. 77–8. The paragraph ends, 'God is love'.

[12] Barth, *The Epistle to the Romans*, pp. 141–2. There again is the Neoplatonic strain which recurs in this tradition.

[13] Pseudo-Dionysius, *The Mystical Theology*, 1033C. The translation is from *Pseudo-Dionysius. The Complete Works*, translated by Colm Luibheid (London: SPCK, 1987), p. 139.

The apparent agnosticism of the negative way masks an almost Promethean aspiration to unity with the divine. 'The way of negation is the way of union.'[14] Dionysius admits as much:

> the words we use about God . . . must not be given the human sense. We should be taken wholly out of ourselves and become wholly of God . . .[15]

That is rather a contrast with the one who did not grasp at divinity, but made himself a servant, and only after that was 'highly exalted'. Once again, we can observe Schleiermacher's essential continuity with this tradition, with his notion of a directly intuited relation to the divine which serves as a modernized version of the unmediated union supposedly to be achieved by ascending from the material to the immaterial.

The third point is that this world-view ought to have been rejected centuries ago on the grounds of a doctrine of creation formed in the light of the Trinity. The interaction of God and the world in Christ, with its implicit affirmation of the goodness of the created world, 'material' as well as 'spiritual', implies a radical critique of the dualism of material and intellectual, sensible and intelligible, which permeates the classical doctrine of the attributes. But without that dualism, the way of ascent becomes impossible, cut off by the 'descent' of Christ – and all its anticipations in the pages of the Old Testament – who makes God known *in* the world, within the structures of space and time, not *by abstraction from* them.

[14] Paul Rorem, *Pseudo-Dionysius. A Commentary on the Texts and an Introduction to Their Influence* (New York and Oxford: Oxford University Press, 1993), pp. 165–6.

[15] Pseudo-Dionysius, *The Divine Names*, 856D. Luibheid, p. 106.

This has important implications for our understanding of theological language, but let us first summarize the argument so far. The chief objection to the theory of predication underlying the negative theology and the way of causality in general is its almost total lack of material and incarnational content. The word 'incarnational' rather than trinitarian is used here because we are sometimes assured that Pseudo-Dionysius and Aquinas are trinitarian in their doctrines of God, though how one can be trinitarian in a development of the attributes that makes neither Christ nor the Spirit constitutive for their construal is a question we must leave to the exponents of the tradition to answer. Moreover, the word 'incarnational' is used in a particular way. It could be said that the derivation of the divine attributes from the Five Ways and their cause–effect conceptuality is incarnational in the general sense of taking the material world seriously.[16] But it is not incarnational in centring itself on the humanity of Jesus and the story of Israel. That is the key to the matter. The humanity of Jesus Christ is redeemed matter, the only truly – eschatologically – redeemed matter. To move to the doctrine of God from there is a rather different matter from setting off from a general doctrine of materiality which has then to be transcended. It is in this light that we move to say something of the theology of language which is at stake in this topic.

III Two Rival Accounts of Predication

As we have seen, the tradition of negative theology commits two offences: on the one hand of intellectual over-

---

[16] That is, if using the material world as a ladder to the immaterial is to take it seriously, which is doubtful.

confidence – in other words, rationalism – of assuming that we know with which concepts to begin and how to refine them to speak of God; and on the other of what can amount to a denial of revelation.[17] We now turn to consider the matter of language. There are two rival accounts of language in contention in the discussion of the language used of divinity. The first begins with the mythical anthropomorphism of the Greek deities and negates it. The emphasis is on removing all traces of contamination by the language of created things. God is not what material things are. While this may indeed be the case, the method operates in such a way as to disable from the outset any use of language which might be seen to be based in God's actual, historical engagement with material reality, and particularly in the humanity of Jesus Christ. Because in this idealistic account God is all mind, intellect tends to be played against imagination, concept against metaphor. That is one problem. The other, as we have seen, is that of analogy. It is not being contested that analogies are part of the process of theological argumentation; rather, that the analogical system which is bound up with a hierarchical metaphysic of reality distorts historic revelation. It is that, I have argued, which applies a stranglehold to the doctrine of God, making secondary or even excluding the attributes derived from God's historical action.

While Duns Scotus is often vilified as the one who ushered in the age of unbelief by his denial of analogy, there is also a case – and we shall see it reinforced in the next chapter – that on the contrary he was one of the exponents of a

---

[17] This seems to be further evidence for the claim that, as in so many topics of theology, the tradition has been contaminated because the Greek philosophical heritage has operated side by side with or even in preference to the Old Testament.

refutation of the Neoplatonic distortion of theology that is so evident in the history of the doctrine of the divine attributes:

> . . . there is no need to make the distinction that we cannot know what God is: we can only know what He is not. For every denial is intelligible only in terms of some affirmation. It is also clear that we can know negations of God only by means of affirmations; for if we deny anything of God, it is because we wish to do away with something inconsistent with what we have already affirmed.

Like Gregory of Nazianzus before him, Scotus is not content with the priority of the negative. The question then is, whence come the affirmations which have to be denied on the grounds of theological consistency? Although, as we shall see in a later chapter, there are places where Scotus shows himself to be a theologian of revelation, in the work from which that citation was taken he is mainly concerned to reverse the order of the traditional scholastic procedures rather than to reject them. In fact, Scotus adopts a version of the way of eminence:

> Every metaphysical inquiry about God proceeds in this fashion: the formal motion of something is considered; the imperfection associated with this notion in creatures is removed, and then, retaining this same formal notion, we ascribe to it the ultimate degree of perfection and then attribute it to God.[18]

---

[18] John Duns Scotus, *The Oxford Commentary*, citations taken from Colin Gunton, Stephen Holmes and Murray Rae, editors, *The Practice of Theology. A Reader* (London: SCM Press, 2001), pp. 295 and 296.

What Scotus has left behind, and he shows that he loses it in his rejection elsewhere of the doctrine that the Platonic forms subsist in the mind of God,[19] is the way of causality as it is understood in the Neoplatonic tradition, and it is that which would appear to be the burden of the complaint against him by those who feel that he has, so to speak, unmoored the world from God. Yet what such critics of Scotus fail to realize is that the way of causality is not the sole possible way of relating God and the world.

A hallmark of Scotus' development is his claim that words are used univocally, not analogically, when they are used of God and the creatures. He has, however, a rather different concept of univocity from Aquinas', not holding that words are used in exactly the same sense of the creator and the created, but that 'that concept [is] univocal which possesses sufficient unity in itself, so that to affirm and deny it of one and the same thing would be a contradiction'.[20] In relation to words used both of creator and of creation, this means that 'every inquiry regarding God is based upon the supposition that the intellect has the same univocal concept which it obtained from the creatures'.[21] As Richard Cross points out, in this light a concept of analogy requires an element of univocity:

> we can give an account of analogy only if we accept that *some* concepts we apply to God and creatures are univocal. These univocal concepts correspond to attributes common in some sense to God and creatures.[22]

[19] See Efrem Bettoni, *Duns Scotus. The Basic Principles of his Philosophy*, translated by B. Bonansea (Westport, Connecticut: Greenwood Press, 1978), p. 154.

[20] Scotus, *The Oxford Commentary*, Gunton, et al., p. 295.

[21] Scotus, *The Oxford Commentary*, Gunton, et al., p. 296.

[22] Richard Cross, *Duns Scotus* (New York and Oxford: Oxford University Press, 1999), pp. 37–8.

It would perhaps not be too crude to say that unless, let us say, the concept of good meant in some way the same in respect to God and to the creatures, there is no way of knowing how it is to be predicated of either.

Suppose that we are even more radical, and suggest that we begin rather with what are called the communicable attributes as they are made known from God's side, and see how things might work. There is a case for saying that the concept of love is used in the same sense of God and of what is expected of human agents, *given that God is creator and redeemer, and we are but creatures and the recipients of redeeming grace.* Suppose that we were to define love – and it is not intended to be a full definition, but enough to make the point – as being and doing for the other what the other needs (when 'needs' include such things as equal regard, assistance in need, and the like). In that case, God's love and ours are precisely the same kind of action, always given that God does not fail in love while we do. And is not that the message of the first letter of John, a text that will prove continually suggestive for our topic? Divine love is a pattern for human love, because it is precisely the same kind of attitude and action. '[S]ince God so loved us, we ought also to love one another' (1 John 4.11). Indeed, there is a sense in which divine love *becomes*, in the Spirit, human love, in that the latter is, in one respect, identical with the former, because it is the former enabled to become God's love in action: 'if we love one another, God lives in us and his love is made complete in us'. Is not that inescapably a form of univocity? (Clearly, the love of the man Jesus *is* the love of God in action, just as his anger at the sickness which disfigures the creation is the wrath of God against evil. This is a theme to which we shall return in the final chapter.) To put it another way: if the Son is the stamp (χαρακτὴρ) of God's substance (ὑποστάσεως!) – the NIV translates 'exact representation of his being' – then should it not follow that something of Scotus' conception of univocity should hold, in his case and *therefore* in ours – when and as God wills? Here we have support from Jewish scholarship. 'The rabbinic principle, "the Torah speaks through human language . . ." is helpful here . . . Revelation comes *to* and *for* us *in* the world . . .'[23]

All this gives us an introduction to a broader conception of theological language than the tradition of negative theology is often able to provide. It is in particular quite astonishing that a whole tradition of theological language has been developed with scarce consideration of the work of the Holy Spirit in empowering language to be what it is created to be. We can agree with the classical tradition of analogical predication in its claim that metaphors in which God is described in terms of created things – rocks, fortresses and women in childbirth – have to be treated as metaphors. The difference is in what we make, theologically, of them. If we must purge our language of all reference to material things, it will need to be rationalized and all references to the created world demythologized by a process of negation, by which is meant, as we have seen, the stripping away of their reference to the created world. As negated, as stripped of material reference, it is then supposed that they are somehow empowered to speak theologically in the way that other words are not ('We know of God only what he is not'). If, on the contrary, we construe all our theological terms as functions of God's involvement through his Son in the created world, in person in Jesus of Nazareth and

[23] David Novak, 'Karl Barth on Divine Command: A Jewish Response', *Scottish Journal of Theology* 54 (2001), 463–83 (474–5).

anticipatorily – but really – in his presences as they are
recorded in the Old Testament, then a different theology of
language is required. The Spirit is the spirit of all the
created order, material and 'spiritual' alike, and is able to
empower language of all kinds, not just philosophically
construed abstractions. We must, for example, consider
such episodes as the angelic visitors to Abraham, according
to which it was 'the Lord' who appeared (Gen. 18); Jacob's
mysterious assailant (Gen. 32); the burning bush (Exod. 3);
angelic visitors to, for example, Manoah and his wife
(Judg. 13), and consider the implications they have for our
language about God.

Suppose, then, that we reject a rationalist account of
language according to which our concepts are in some way
already qualified to speak of divine things so long as any
contamination by materiality is expunged, what might a
pneumatological approach to the meaning of our words
imply for a theology of the divine attributes?

1. Words, all words, are created realities. None of them
is from the outset qualified to describe divine being, even,
or rather especially, abstract words like 'being'. Words are
therefore things, so that it is worth citing Coleridge: 'I would
endeavour to destroy the old antithesis of *Words and
Things*, elevating, as it were, words into Things, & living
Things, too.'[24] That is to pick up something of the sense of
words as achieving ends to be found in such passages as
Isaiah 55.10–11. They are things used by those beings,
created in the image of God, who articulate them by means
of the physical apparatus of brain, vocal chords and ink. As
Barth rightly comments, all words are anthropomorphic in

---

[24] Samuel Taylor Coleridge, Letter to Goodwin, 22 September 1800.
Selected Letters, edited by H. J. Jackson (Oxford: Clarendon Press,
1987), p. 79.

that sense.[25] Positively, we can understand them not as in some way representing immaterial forms, but as the vehicles of our indwelling in and engagement with material reality, that material reality in which the Son of God has taken up his dwelling, and lives to make intercession for us.

2. Words are those realities by which the Holy Spirit enables created intellects, sometimes, when and as God pleases, to articulate the truth of the creator and his creation. In the one definitive and exemplary case, the ministry of Jesus, God accommodates himself to our condition and by his Spirit enables the one human being truly in his image to be and to articulate the truth (in physical acts and parables, it must be noted). The implication for us is that through him, and through him alone, the Spirit enables us to speak truly of God's eternal being, both as it is revealed in time and as it is in eternity. It is here also that we find some purchase for a Scotist claim about the univocity of language in speaking of both the creator and the creation. We might venture: Jesus' parables *are* the self-presentation of God in worldly language.

3. Human beings are fallen beings, who can articulate the truth, either of the world or of God, only by a kind of redemption of their created faculties. Let us pause to consider the effect of sin on human cognitional faculties. Sin is structurally the disruption of the human relation to God which at the human level takes the form of idolatry: that is to say, a confusion of creature and creator of such a kind that although the created world everywhere witnesses to the hand that made it, fallen human beings cannot without more ado simply find the right language to engage the world as it really is. It is not yet as it will be, and enabled

---

[25] Barth, *Church Dogmatics*, 2/1, p. 222.

to be so only through redemption; and the same is the case with the language we use of it. To repeat a previous point in a different context: to suppose that this can be done merely by negating what we suppose to be the nature of created reality is rationalistically to suppose that this condition can be evaded. The doctrine of sin rules that out absolutely. That is the negative aspect. The positive is that, as Jüngel has shown in speaking of Barth's theology, revelation enables a gain to language of such a kind that it is empowered by God to speak of him.[26] It is that conception which we shall be able to develop if, instead of concentrating on the negations, and the other doctrines of the way of causality, we turn instead to the biblical account of God's interaction with the world, and the trinitarian account of divine action which it makes possible.

Before returning to the main thread of our argument, we can now conclude this chapter by saying that the doctrine of the divine attributes is devoted to seeking an account of which created words, and in what way, can be supposed to be the least inadequate to characterize the being of God. In that respect and in that alone it is to couch the relation between creator and creation in terms not so much of *an* analogy as of a range of analogies, some of which will be metaphorical in form, of such a kind that God's acts license and empower a theology of his being. To be true to that, we must be far more open and eclectic than has been the tradition about the variety of forms of language that we use. In the next chapters, we shall explore something of what the doctrine of the Trinity might have to offer. What we shall find in particular is that when, at the time of the Reformation, a more biblical account of the divine being

---

[26] *Sprachgewinn.* Eberhard Jüngel, *Gottes Sein ist in Werden* (Tübingen: J. C. B. Mohr (Paul Siebeck), 1966, second edition), p. 22.

was attempted, a greater ambivalence and unclarity often resulted, because the two traditions began to live uncomfortably side by side, with a loss rather than gain in clarity and consistence.

5

Towards a Trinitarian Reading of the Tradition. 1. The Relevance of the 'Economic' Trinity

I Illustrations from the Fathers and Schoolmen

What difference does the Trinity make? The question divides into two. First, the question of the economy: of what happens when the doctrine of the divine attributes takes shape in the light of the economy of God's actions – of creation, reconciliation and redemption. To review some of the questions will be the burden of this short chapter. Referring back to the previous chapters, we can say that if the tradition goes wrong in so far as it believes that it can discover the shape of God's being by negating the supposed characteristics of the material or visible world, a trinitarian construction will begin with the implications of the Son's involvement in the material world. What does this tell us about the divine attributes? The second question is: What is the relation between what we say about the triune God – God in his eternal being – and the divine attributes? That will be the topic of Chapter 6. We shall see that the two questions are complementary as we follow the path marked out by Barth's determination to identify God from and in his acts. God is what he does, and does what he is. As we shall see, this is not to identify the doctrines of the economic and eternal Trinities in the direct way that is sometimes done by those who have come under the influence of the so-called 'Rahner's rule', but to restrict our claims for our knowledge of who God is to those things licensed by what he actually does. All depends upon a satisfactory answer to the question: Who *is* God in his *act*? Thus, while the first question concerns the relation of God's act and his being, the second is about his being and, accordingly, the attributes which are revealed in action. If God *is* in his act, then the questions are essentially the same, or different aspects of the same.

This chapter will be devoted primarily to the first of the two questions, and is introduced with a brief account of what is meant by God's action, by which I mean personal and intentional acts designed to bring about some purpose or change in the world. (It would be helpful if 'act' could be defined in some other terms, but that is difficult, because of the basic character of the concept. 'Something brought about by a personal / intentional agent . . . ' simply repeats the point.) Acts are identified by their outcome in the world, by what happens by means of them. Central among what we call God's acts are such things as creation, salvation and redemption, the beginning, centre and end of God's relation to what is not himself. While a full account and defence cannot be given here, the situation can be stated in a Cappadocian summary: that all of God's acts take their beginning in the Father, are put into effect through the Son and reach their completion in the Spirit. Put otherwise, God's actions are *mediated*: he brings about his purposes towards and in the world by the mediating actions of the Son and the Spirit, his 'two hands'. Rather schematically, it can be said the Son is the focus of God the Father's

immanent action, his involvement *within* the structures of
the world, as paradigmatically in Jesus, but also in his
various angelic and other presences to the world recorded in
the Old Testament. That is why Paul's piece of rabbinic
exegesis in 1 Corinthians 10.4 is not fanciful but realistic:
'for they [Israel in the wilderness] drank from the spiritual
rock that accompanied them, and that rock was Christ'. By
contrast, the Spirit, as the one by whose agency the Father
makes the creation perfect in his Son, is the focus of transcendent, eschatological action, pulling things forward to
that for which God has made them. The tradition of negative theology is brought into question here because the identification of God is by his action both in and for the sake of
the whole created world, 'material' and 'spiritual' alike,
rather than by the denial of the material features of createdness. When such considerations form the focus, the divine
attributes are understood rather differently.

One interesting way to understand this point is by
observing some of the places in the tradition where,
albeit not always explicitly, trinitarian considerations have
subverted, or have shown signs of subverting, the dominant
theology. As we can now see more clearly than they could,
all the early theologians are marked by the theology of the
Greeks. (Similarly, later generations will no doubt be
equally conscious of the way modern presuppositions,
many of them not all that different from the Greek, have
shaped our theology.) Some, however, went further than
others in subverting the largely negative theology which
was the main focus of so many of their assumptions about
the being of God. We shall take two main patristic examples, Irenaeus and Gregory of Nazianzus, and then move on
to take soundings of later revealing historical developments.

Irenaeus shares many of the characteristics of Greek theology, including a tendency to conceive God in terms of intellect:

> The Father . . . a simple uncompounded Being . . . altogether like and equal to Himself, since He is wholly understanding and wholly spirit, and wholly thought and wholly intelligence and wholly reason, and wholly hearing and wholly seeing, etc.[1]

and:

> God is all mind, all reason, all active spirit, all light . . . such feelings and divisions [of operations] cannot be ascribed to Him.[2]

Irenaeus' leaning towards the abstract derives from his assault on the grossly anthropomorphic imagery of the Gnostics, who did indeed make many of their deities little more than magnified human beings. Yet always such apparent abstractions are glossed by a strong affirmation that God is the creator, just as we found the author of Isaiah 40 glossing with a concrete comparison his apparent denial that there is anything to which God can be compared.

Above all significant about Irenaeus is that, by virtue of his reading of the involvement of the Son of God in the world – the economy of God's *material* actions as recorded in both Old and New Testaments – he refuses to be content with the old definitions, and so subverts them. Irenaeus denies the attributes projected by his opponents in order to preserve his trinitarian theology of a God made known in the economy of his action in creation and salvation, an economy which is the very heartbeat of his theology.

[1] Irenaeus, *Haer.*, 2. 13. 3.
[2] Irenaeus, *Haer.*, 2. 28. 4.

As Osborn suggests, alluding to what he calls 'a form of horizontal Platonism', 'Irenaeus presents a continuous history . . . where sources of knowledge are given through prophets and apostles to provide knowledge of truth.'[3] It is, as a matter of fact, rather more than that, for it is not only sources of knowledge that are given but descriptions – indeed, *mediations* – of redemptive action. It must therefore be affirmed that what we have is not a transposition but a critique of Platonism. What have been called the 'horizontal', the historical sources of knowledge, change everything. For christological reasons, therefore, Irenaeus challenges the theology of the divine unknowing. He presents a highly qualified form of the doctrine of God's unknowability, effectively subverting it:

> that God cannot be known without God: but this is the express will of God, that God should be known.[4]

Indeed, the Father is made visible through the Son:

> all saw the Father in the Son: for the Father is the invisible of the Son, but the Son is the visible of the Father .[5]

The subversion of any static or mainly cosmological account of the attributes is made clear in one wonderful and much-cited christological passage. The emphasis is on action:

> He took man up into Himself, the invisible becoming visible, the incomprehensible being made comprehensible, the impassible becoming capable of suffering, and

[3] Eric Osborn, *Irenaeus of Lyons* (Cambridge: Cambridge University Press, 2001), p. 15. It is indeed so horizontal as to be scarcely describable as Platonism, in view of the Platonic tendency to deny that anything historical and material can be the source of knowledge; rather such a thing can be only the ground of opinion.

[4] Irenaeus, *Haer.*, 4. 6. 4.

[5] Irenaeus, *Haer.*, 4. 6. 6.

the Word being made man . . . so that as in super-celestial, spiritual and invisible things, the Word of God is supreme, so also in things visible and corporeal He might possess the supremacy . . .[6]

One only has to read a short way in Irenaeus to notice that this theologian is interested in divine action, and in divine being only as support for that:

For with Him were always present the Word and Wisdom, the Son and the Spirit, by whom and in whom, freely and spontaneously, He made all things . . .[7]

Again and again the attributes are treated in the light of the *act* of creation:

But there is only one God, the Creator . . . He is Father, He is God, He the Founder, He the Maker, He the Creator, who made those things by Himself, that is, through His Word and Wisdom . . . He is just; He is good. . . . He is the God of Abraham, and the God of Isaac, and the God of Jacob, the God of the living . . . He is the Father of our Lord Jesus Christ . . .[8]

In theory, Irenaeus is as insistent as the Greeks that God is 'above [all] these properties and therefore indescribable'.[9] And yet he describes him, and the list of attributes he gives soon afterwards suggests that he has drawn on scripture more than on the negations of the philosophers: 'intelligence, word, life, incorruption, truth, wisdom, goodness, and such like'.[10]

---

[6] Irenaeus, *Haer.*, 3. 16. 6.
[7] Irenaeus, *Haer.*, 4. 20. 1.
[8] Irenaeus, *Haer.*, 2. 30. 9.
[9] Irenaeus, *Haer.*, 2. 13. 4.
[10] Irenaeus, *Haer.*, 2. 13. 9.

In his *Second Theological Oration*, Gregory of Nazianzus deploys a number of arguments against the Eunomians, arguments that are interestingly parallel to Irenaeus' points against the Gnostics. Eunomianism is, roughly speaking, the doctrine that because we know that God is (*must be*) ingenerate or unbegotten, an orthodox trinitarianism is impossible. The argument is partly one from one divine attribute, simplicity:

> For two to share the essence of the unbegotten One would mean division / separation and this would be unworthy of God since God is altogether free from composition. Furthermore, such division would prompt thought about God as occupying space, which is also inappropriate.[11]

That is to say, orthodox christology is ruled out on the grounds of an a priori doctrine of divine simplicity. For our purposes, we can see that Eunomius (in that respect, no different from some of the negative theologians we have met) appears to have great confidence that he knows what God can and cannot be. He represents, that is to say, a form of rationalism, and it is this which Cappadocian assertions of the unknowability of God are designed to refute. However, because the Cappadocians are, to use a modern way of putting it, theologians of revelation, Gregory also recognizes the limits of a purely negative theology:

> But a man who states what God is not without going on to say what He is, acts much in the same way as one would who when asked how many twice five make, should answer, 'Not two, nor three (etc.)' . . . but would

---

[11] Mark W. Elliott, 'Eunomius (c. 335–394)', in Trevor Hart, editor, *The Dictionary of Historical Theology* (Carlisle: Paternoster Press, 2000), p. 193.

not answer 'ten', nor settle the mind of his questioner on the firm ground of the answer. For, [he continues significantly] it is much easier, and more concise, to shew what a thing is not from what it is, than to demonstrate what it is by stripping it of what it is not.[12]

Gregory's negative arguments are largely designed to cut down the pretensions of human reason, and I cite him again because of the interesting use he makes of the attributes of impassibility and incomprehensibility:

[T]he Divine Nature cannot be apprehended by human reason, and . . . we cannot even represent to ourselves all its greatness. And this is not out of envy [Gregory knows his Greek religion!], for envy is far from the Divine Nature, which is passionless, and only good and Lord of all. . . . Nor yet is this incomprehensibility for the sake of His own glory and honour . . . as if His possession of His glory and majesty depended on the impossibility of approaching Him.[13]

The final sentence is rather obscure, but seems to be looking for a positive meaning for the doctrine of the incomprehensibility of God. It suggests that for Gregory God's incomprehensibility serves for the sake of creaturely knowledge, rather, it would seem, like Calvin's doctrine of accommodation, according to which God in scripture accommodates himself to the measure of our understanding. Gregory's negations are controlled by the gospel of the revelatory knowledge of God which is not to be subverted by an abstract rationalism of unknowability. That this is

---

[12] Gregory of Nazianzus, *Second Theological Oration*, 9. Nicene and Post-Nicene Fathers (Edinburgh: T. & T. Clark, 1989), vol. 7, pp. 291–2.

[13] Gregory, *Second Theological Oration*, 10, p. 292.

not simply an imposition of a 'modern' doctrine of revelation is made clear by the fact that Gregory can speak of those who are 'eyewitnesses and spectators of His unsearchable judgements'.[14]

Admittedly, the use he makes of biblical revelation is sometimes rather insubstantial, nugatory even, so that towards the end of this theological oration he simply goes off on a natural theological ramble about the wonders of nature, etc. Yet on the way there are signs of a more positive theology at work. Perhaps the most interesting trinitarian hints are in the appeal he makes to what Irenaeus would have seen as Old Testament appearances of Christ, for example when Jacob 'wrestled with God in human form' and the visit of the angel to Manoah and his wife.[15] Yet they remain hints, and he makes little substantively of the matter. Indeed, the loss of a secure christological construal of the doctrine of the divine attributes left things open to the development of the negative rationalism which we met in the previous chapter. For the most part, despite his own warning, so far as the attributes are concerned Gregory did tend to 'state what God is not without going on to say what he is'. (At least so far as what we have come to call the divine attributes are concerned. He had much to say about the identification of God as Father, Son and Spirit; but, as we shall see, a satisfactory doctrine of God also requires the identification of the kind of agency in which the triune God interacts with his world.) What we learn to our profit is his rejection of rationalism and the kind of assistance which a more trinitarian approach might offer.

Our third example is a medieval one, and comes from

---

[14] Gregory, *Second Theological Oration*, 12, p. 292.
[15] Gregory, *Second Theological Oration*, 18–19, pp. 294–5.

Duns Scotus, the first late-medieval theologian to begin to question the negative theology. According to the author of a recent article, Scotus began a move away from the cosmological causal pattern deriving from Proclus, a move that was later completed by Ockham. This represented a rejection both of a hierarchical language in favour of a trinitarian one and of the distinction made by Lombard and the Fourth Lateran Council between the being and the *personalität* (personal character) of God.[16] This separation of being and person is a crucial one, and, as we shall see, continued in the Reformation tradition. Scotus' unique contribution is to be seen in his reconstruction of the doctrine of divine infinity. Aquinas had defined infinity as the removal of creaturely limitations, arriving at 'a negative concept in analogical manner'.[17] Against this, Scotus no longer sought God as in the Neoplatonic tradition 'behind the creation. God reveals himself *in* the creation.'[18] Scotus thus rejected all *unmediated* conceptualizing of God, and arrived at a definition of infinity in terms of intensity, a conception closely linked to a trinitarian understanding of the relation of God and the world. God's infinity is to be found in the positive richness of his being, and not primarily in the absence of limit, whether spatial or temporal.[19] (A similar point is made by Robert Jenson in conversation with Gregory of Nyssa. 'In Aristotle's understanding, something

[16] Klaus Bannach, 'Das Unendliche bei Duns Scotus', *Neue Zeitschrift für Systematische Theologie und Religionsphilosophie* 43 (2001), 281–99 (281).

[17] Bannach, 'Das Unendliche', 286–7.

[18] Bannach, 'Das Unendliche', 287.

[19] Bannach, 'Das Unendliche', 293–4. See especially 293: 'Gegen Aristoteles oder an ihm vorbei behauptet Scotus, dass es auch eine Unendlichkeit der Intensität gibt.' As we have seen in Chapter 4, this is of a piece with Scotus' assault on the priority of the negative way of knowing God. It is a matter of an a posteriori as against a priori theology also.

would be infinite because it *lacked* all boundaries; Gregory's God is infinite because he *overcomes* all boundaries.'[20])

And so with the figure of Scotus, whose long-term influence included that of John Calvin, we move to the Reformation and post-Reformation era. Illuminating about Calvin, as with his successors, is the way in which a double tug continues to operate. The place where the worst influence of Calvin's theology is often discerned is in the fact that he appears, like Augustine before him, to have placed the divine double decree of election and reprobation prior to the revelation of God's gracious and saving action in Christ, in the mysterious unknowability of God. Whether or not that is fair, and it is not entirely so, Calvin's place in the tradition of negative theology is unquestionable, at least in showing one of its worst symptoms. A definite ambivalence is to be observed in Calvin's treatment of the attributes. On the one hand, it is firmly based on biblical representations of God's actions. Calvin's account derives from an observation of what he calls God's powers. 'Now we hear the same powers enumerated there [in scripture] that we have noted as shining in heaven and earth: kindness, goodness, mercy, justice, judgment, and truth.' These, he rightly avers, all witness to God's eternity and self-existence. And yet Calvin takes away with one hand what he has given with the other. 'Thereupon his powers are mentioned, by which he is shown to us not as he is in himself, but as he is toward us.' Calvin's motives for so speaking are of the best: 'so that this recognition of him consists more in living experience than in vain and high-

[20] Robert W. Jenson, *Systematic Theology*, volume 1, *The Triune God*; volume 2, *The Works of God* (New York and Oxford: Oxford University Press, 1997, 1999), vol. 1, p. 216.

flown speculation'.[21] And yet, if God's self-revelation is not of himself as he is in his eternal triune love, is there not a danger that a wedge has been inserted, so that the revelation of God in act is subverted by foreign accounts of his being? An equally appropriate metaphor might be that of the Trojan horse, for some such disaster did occur in the following centuries.

II The Relevance of the 'Economic' Trinity. 2. Reformed Theology

The tradition of Reformed dogmatic theology is interesting – as we have already seen in the passage cited from Braun in the first chapter – in representing side by side what appear to be little more than repetitions of scholastic patterns and implicit criticism of them. The era of the so-called Protestant scholasticism is sometimes seen as one in which a return was made to the kind of Aristotelian conceptuality which had been rejected by the Reformers.[22] While that is an oversimplification, there are signs in the treatment of the attributes that something like that is indeed the case. Some of Calvin's successors proceed as if nothing in this sphere had changed as the result of his theology. Biblical representations of divine action which had for him altered the conception of divine being sometimes appear to be irrelevant. It is almost as if, rightly feeling that dogmatic theology required a more systematic treatment of the attributes than

[21] All citations are from John Calvin, *Institutes of the Christian Religion*, I. 10. 2, edited by J. T. McNeill, translated and indexed by F. L. Battles (Philadelphia: Westminster Press, 1960), 2 vols., Library of Christian Classics, vol. 20, pp. 97–8.

[22] See Ronald N. Frost, 'Aristotle's *Ethics*: The Real Reason for Luther's Reformation?', *Trinity Journal* NS 18 (1997), 223–41.

he had offered, Calvin's successors had nowhere to go – or went nowhere – but to the stream of pre-Reformation tradition.

Yet one crucial positive development is highly instructive, and to see what had changed for some of this tradition, however, let us recall part of Hodge's list of the divine attributes. 'God is a Spirit, infinite, eternal, and unchangeable, in his being, wisdom, power, holiness, justice, goodness and truth.' The first three we have met often enough, and they represent the almost universal tendency to begin with, if not actual negations, then abstractions. It is the presence in the list of holiness which marks a departure, for, as we saw, it did not appear in Aquinas' treatment of the attributes. There seems to be little doubt that its presence is the result of Reformation, and particularly Calvin's, emphasis of the doctrine of sanctification.[23] If making holy is one of God's prominent acts, then holiness might appear to be an important attribute, especially as it appears to be so in scripture and is the defining epithet of God the Spirit. But the hint was often ignored. Two examples of the failure to develop a new starting point for construction will serve. First: 'In Ames' discussions of the divine attributes, he distils four: "Simplicity, immutability, eternity and immeasurableness" '.[24] Similar is Johannes Wollebius (1586–1629) of Basel. Wollebius is not a negative theologian, at least not in his stated method; yet in content, the outcome is interestingly familiar, especially when it is viewed in the light of Bannach's remarks on Scotus. Propositions 2 and 3 of Book 1 read as follows: 'God is known in himself and in his

[23] For this and several following points I am indebted to the research of Rufus Burton.

[24] Rufus T. Burton, research paper from December 2001. The reference is to W. Ames, *The Marrow of Theology*, 1. 4. 50.

works. He is known in himself absolutely in his essence, relatively in the persons.' That distinction between the absolute attributes of God's being and the relative attributes of the persons is one to which we must come but, like our author, we must first tarry briefly with his succinct and unexceptionable definition of the attributes 'by which he [God] offers knowledge of himself to us . . . and by which he is distinguished from the creatures'; and then with his enumeration of the attributes.

> 1. The attributes of the first kind are simplicity and infinity. Immutability and perfection may be added, but they are merely corollaries to simplicity and infinity. . . . [Notice here that God's perfection is a corollary of his simplicity, and not the reverse.]
> 3. The properties of the second kind are life, which is attributed to God in essence, will, attributed to him in commanding, and power, attributed to him in acting.

Again we might note the absence of holiness and love in these lists which, we recall, appear at the outset of the presentation and therefore set the tone of the remaining theology.[25] But, as we shall see, it is the astonishing contradistinction of the absolute and relative attributes which most reveal the rift at the heart of the tradition.

Let us approach our discussion with a contribution from the work of the seventeenth-century Presbyterian, Stephen Charnock, one or two of whose developments enable us to see something of the point of the reference to trinitarian action. In his first volume Charnock shares the twofold approach of Wollebius. He opens his treatise with an account of the essence of God, and indeed begins with a

[25] John W. Beardslee III, editor, *Reformed Dogmatics. J. Wollebius, G. Voetius, F. Turretin* (Grand Rapids: Baker, 1977), pp. 37–9.

centrally biblical concept, God as Spirit. The treatment of this, however, is determined negatively. To affirm that God is a Spirit, he argues, is to deny corporeality and other such features of his being.[26] 'When we say God is a Spirit, it is to be understood by way of negation'.[27] Similar is the discussion of eternity, which 'is a negative attribute'.[28] The gain so far is mainly in the starting definition: to identify God as essentially Spirit is at least an advance on the hierarchical causality beloved of the tradition since Pseudo-Dionysius, and indeed as a result of Charnock's biblical orientation many interesting things are said in the extensive treatment of the topic. Similarly, many of the other attributes which are treated are more strongly biblical in content than those we have frequently met: wisdom, dominion, patience and, above all, holiness. Charnock has rightly seen that the last of the list is crucial and central, and gives an illuminating and perceptive account, steeped in the scriptural narrative of God's actions. The power of the account derives largely from the fact that there is no tradition of a source for the doctrine other than scripture, so that what we read is an account of God's holiness entirely derived from the shape God's action takes in the witness of the Old and New Testaments. The purity, beauty, power and perfection of God show that God's actions are determined by his holiness,[29] while it is also 'An essential and necessary perfection: he is essentially and necessarily holy.'[30]

---

[26] Stephen Charnock, *The Existence and Attributes of God* (Grand Rapids: Baker, 2000), vol. 1, p. 178.

[27] Charnock, *The Existence and Attributes of God*, vol. 1, p. 181.

[28] Charnock, *The Existence and Attributes of God*, vol. 1, p. 281.

[29] 'Without it, his patience would be an indulgence to sin, his mercy a fondness, his wrath a madness, his power a tyranny, his wisdom an unworthy subtilty', vol. 2, pp. 113–14.

[30] Charnock, *The Existence and Attributes of God*, vol. 2, p. 115.

And yet we see in other parts of this great treatise that the method continues to constrain the content, so that although in places, indeed in many places, the content breaks through, grave structural deficiencies remain. A salient instance is to be seen in the treatment of 'The Wisdom of God', where the structural weakness deriving from Wollebius' distinction between attributes 'absolutely in [God's] essence, relatively in the persons' has the following results. Prominent is that although Charnock recognizes that the Son of God is 'Wisdom in himself', he is not conceived as being essential to God's eternal wisdom, but, it would appear, only to the way that wisdom works itself out in time. He is merely the 'personal wisdom . . . because he opens to us the secrets of God', 'personal' here being in some way separate – rather than merely distinct! – from essence. And then a strange argument is appended: 'If the Son were that wisdom whereby the Father is wise, the Son would be also the essence whereby the Father is God.'[31] But is that, a Sabellian conflation of the Father and the Son, the only alternative? If God's wisdom is understood not to be essentially different from his action, but to be revealed in it, then what is the objection to saying that the eternal Son is the wisdom whereby God's wisdom is his wise action, because it is that which takes place in the career of Jesus? To put it another way, we might ask whether to see the Son as God's wisdom is mere appropriation or attribution, and not rather a revelation of the very essence of God.

The outcome of this foreshortening of vision is that Charnock fails to take up the biblical teaching according to which *Jesus* is the wisdom of God in action. The only allusion to 1 Corinthians 2 in this context is to 2.7, 'No, we

---

[31] Charnock, *The Existence and Attributes of God*, vol. 1, pp. 508–9.

speak of God's secret wisdom, a wisdom that has been hidden . . .'. According to Charnock, God's wisdom is thereby shown to be incomprehensible wisdom, 'wisdom in a mystery',[32] but that is reading the text negatively, against the grain of Paul's discussion. For Paul, by contrast, 'mystery' is used of something revealed: a 'secret and hidden' wisdom of which Paul *speaks* (λαλοῦμεν), and it is only hidden to some ('the rulers of this age', vv. 6 and 7). This *revealed* wisdom is, as the earlier argument makes clear, Jesus and his cross; and, as Paul says later in the same chapter, something which is given by the Spirit, 'who searches . . . even the depths of God' (v. 10). 'This is what we speak . . . in words taught by the Spirit, expressing spiritual things to the spiritual (πνευματικοῖς πνευματικὰ)' (v. 13).[33] Christology and pneumatology make all of the difference, but scarcely shape Charnock's treatment of this particular attribute.

The reason for the blindness to what is actually said in scripture can only be attributed to the dead hand of the negative theology, still resting heavily on the tradition. What we see happening especially in the passage from Wollebius is the effective division of God's being from the persons of the Trinity. That is the effect of distinguishing between the absolute and relative attributes, and more significantly of attributing the difference to that between the essence and the persons. What Calvin adopted from his predecessors has become a disastrous breach between an essence of God, unknowable and indeed impersonal, and

---

[32] Charnock, *The Existence and Attributes of God*, vol. 1, pp. 553–4

[33] Charnock appeals also to 1 Tim. 3.16, but makes the same error of abstraction. In that text, 'great is the mystery of godliness' is succeeded by a statement of christological revelation. Charnock, *The Existence and Attributes*, vol. 1, p. 560.

the personal actions in which God presents himself to us. Is then God, really, deep-down impersonal? Can we then truly rely on what he reveals to us in his triune action? Nor is this simply a matter of a now long-outlived Reformed dogmatics. The effects are with us still. For example, a recent study of Darwin has blamed much of the theological scepticism both shaping the work and descending from it on the negative theology, a natural theology which assumes that it knows who and what God cannot be and do.[34] Similarly, much has recently been said about the way in which negative theologies lie behind much of the theology of projection that is so fashionable in the present. There lies disaster. Nice, polite westerners may project a deity who is moderately feminist and in favour of ecological responsibility and all worthy things, but if the matter is down to the one who projects, there is no end to the demons which can be let loose. Salvation depends on the unflinching affirmation that the God who meets us in the Son and the Spirit is the only God there is.

[34] Cornelius G. Hunter, *Darwin's God. Evolution and the Problem of Evil* (Grand Rapids: Brazos Books, 2001).

6

Towards a Trinitarian Reading of the Tradition. 2. The Relevance of the 'Eternal' Trinity

I Towards a Narrative Definition

We now approach an answer to the question of what our doctrine of the immanent or eternal Trinity, God in himself, might have to teach us about the attributes. The distinction between the doctrines of the economic and eternal or immanent Trinities is important. It is not suggesting that there are two Gods, two Trinities, but that two different things have to be said about the triune God if we are to do justice to scripture: that he is triune as he presents himself to us in our time, and that this tri-unity is eternal. We need to know and say this because we need to know that we can rely on what God reveals: that what he seems to be, that he truly is. Otherwise, how could we rely on his always being loving, holy, merciful, powerful and the rest?

As has already been said, the doctrine of the Trinity performs, among other things, the function of identifying God: with indicating what makes him distinctively who he is. It is a kind of definition. Now, to be sure, when that is said, questions will begin to be raised. Is God the kind of being who can be defined? Is not such an enterprise as this precisely what the negative theology was rightly devised to prevent? The answer is that definition comes in a number of forms. It can be logical – a real essence, in Locke's terms – and claim a measure of completeness, as when we define a triangle as a plane figure consisting of three straight lines in a certain relation to one another; or as when Eunomius defines God a priori in terms of a certain conception of simplicity. A definition can also be ostensive, definition by indication, as we say to a child who is learning to identify colours, that and that and that are red. Again, a definition can be open, in the sense of indicating some of the things characteristic of a person or thing, but never exhaustive – Locke's nominal essence. Thus, speaking of someone's character, we can only begin to list the salient characteristics, knowing that the mystery of the person always eludes final definition. It is something of this kind with which we are concerned here. We know from – for example – a good biography that we can learn a great deal about another human being. A biography is a kind of definition by narrative, yet the narrative is not the whole. In an adequate biography it will constitute also the grounds for an account of character, by which is meant something impressed by the life on the basic material which was given at birth, so that at the end we can make an at least provisional judgment on the kind of person with whom we are dealing. Giving us the freedom to make such a judgment about God is the function of the doctrine of the immanent Trinity.

Is God defined in scripture, and how? Can we attempt generalizations? The point of Paul's account of the divine wisdom in 1 Corinthians 2 is that in the cross of Jesus God defines himself by a particular form of action and that self-definition is apprehensible by the Spirit's gift. Generalizing, we can say that in scripture God is presented both narratively and credally: in narratives of actions and in credal summaries of the meaning of those actions, summaries which were developed and systematized in the early centuries of the church's life. To neglect the first is to risk taking the definition out of its historical placing; to neglect the second is to risk losing any account of the being of God. The foregoing account of the struggle which has taken place in the history of theology between abstract and narrative versions of the doctrine of the attributes is designed to recommend a more strongly narrative approach to the topic, seeking to save theology from an a priori definition in the interests of a doctrine in which being and act are brought into a more successful harmony than appears often to have been the case. It is in that light that we can understand the disaster represented by the distinction drawn by Wollebius: 'God . . . is known in himself absolutely in his essence, relatively in the persons.'[1] Do we not see drawn here in sharpest lines one of the symptoms of western modalism? The essence of God is known pre- and extra-trinitarianly; once that is sketched in, we treat the attributes deriving from the persons. (If Bannach is right, something like that had already been pointed out by Scotus some centuries earlier.)

In recent times, the struggle to develop a more narratively based account of God's attributes has often centred on the doctrine of impassibility, which appears to rule out some of the things done by God, for example genuinely suffering on the cross and being genuinely compassionate with those who suffer. Something will be said about that contentious attribute in the next chapter. Now, however, let us develop our more general theme by a visit to the thought of one who

[1] See above, Chapter 5, p. 88–9.

has been claimed to have re-integrated act and being in a way that goes back to near the roots of trinitarian theology in Athanasius.[2] As Jüngel has shown in his recently re-translated *Gottes Sein ist im Werden – God's Being is in Becoming* – Barth uses the concept of divine becoming to show that there is no breach between God's action and his being. In the incarnation God demonstrates his freedom 'to become unlike Himself and yet to remain the same',[3] and it is this revelation of himself which ought to be the source of any conclusions we draw about what he is in eternity. That is the order of knowing: we know God (by his ostensive self-definition) from and in his acts. We know *who* God is from what he does. The other aspect of our response to the same divine self-presentation in time is that the order of being grounds the order of knowing, so that what God does in time is shown to be a function of what he is in eternity. The outcome is that historical revelation and eternal being correspond to one another:

> The self-relatedness of God's being makes possible God's self-interpretation [his self-definition, we might say]. God *reveals* himself *as* Father, Son and Spirit because he *is* God *as* Father, Son and Spirit.[4]

Barth certainly distinguishes God's 'essence as the One who works and reveals himself' from the 'essence of God as such'. But this distinction has no other purpose than

[2] T. F. Torrance, *Karl Barth. An Introduction to his Early Theology* (London: SCM Press, 1962).

[3] Karl Barth, *Church Dogmatics*, translation edited by G. W. Bromiley and T .F. Torrance (Edinburgh: T. & T. Clark, 1957–1975), I/1, p. 320.

[4] Eberhard Jüngel, *God's Being is in Becoming. The Trinitarian Being of God in the Theology of Karl Barth*, translated with a new Introduction by John Webster (Edinburgh: T. & T. Clark, 2001), p. 42.

to establish the fact that God reveals himself 'not constrained by His essence', but 'in a free decision grounded
in His essence'. . . . But the essence of this one who works
is now thought strictly from the point of view of revelation, and so not as substance, but as the 'unity of Father,
Son and Spirit among themselves' to which 'their unity
ad extra' corresponds.[5]

Barth's project to bring revelation and being together is an
implicit, and often explicit, reproach to much of the tradition.
It establishes an important principle: that treatments of the
being or essence of God must be trinitarian from the outset
and that it must be a trinitarianism which is based in, and a
drawing out of the implications of, the economic Trinity: of
how God reveals himself to be in the narratively identified
economy of creation, reconciliation and redemption.

In this light, we move to sketch the main lines of the way
in which this trinitarian construal comes to shape Barth's
own discussion of the divine perfections.[6] Beginning with
the claim that 'God is means God loves', Barth proceeds to
give an account of the divine perfections in the light of the
kind of love that is revealed in scripture.[7] It is love that is
given freely to those who are and cannot but be unworthy
of it. This unconstrained love for the unworthy other
provides in turn the basis of a polarity or dialectic of love
and freedom which forms a matrix within which the
discussion of the attributes is formed. Barth begins with
a polar account of God's being: God loves, but he loves

---

[5] Jüngel, *God's Being*, p. 47.

[6] As a matter of fact, Barth's very creativity in this one of the finest
sections of his dogmatics has brought a number of problems in its train,
at the extremes threatening to collapse the orders of time and of eternity
rather than relating them positively.

[7] Barth, *Church Dogmatics*, 2/1, p. 283.

freely, so that each of the perfections is to be understood as characterized as a perfection either of love or of freedom, but in such a way that perfections of God's loving are understood in the light of freedom, perfections of his freedom in the light of his love. God's attributes are thus treated dialectically as functions of the freedom in which God is love and loves the world. Barth is insistent that this is not a division of a kind that suggests that while love is the seeking of fellowship freedom is God's transcendence over against the created world. Rather, all the perfections are an expression at once of God's love and freedom:

> God is not first the One who loves, and then somewhere and somehow, in contradistinction to that, the One who is also free. And when He loves He does not surrender His freedom, but exercises it in a supreme degree.[8]

There are twelve perfections, the first six being three perfections of the divine loving (grace, mercy and patience) which are dialectically paired with and whose meaning is therefore controlled by the perfections of the divine freedom (holiness, righteousness and wisdom). An example of the integration of act and being is Barth's account of grace and holiness:

> Grace is the distinctive mode of God's being in so far as it seeks and creates fellowship. . . . We are not [Barth qualifies six pages later] . . . making any crucial change of theme when we go on to speak of God's holiness. . . . As holy, [grace] is characterised by the fact that God, as He seeks and creates fellowship, is always the Lord. . . .

---

[8] Barth, *Church Dogmatics*, 2/1, pp. 344–5.

He condemns, excludes and annihilates all contradiction and resistance to it.[9]

After the six perfections of love that is free, there follow three perfections of the divine freedom (unity, constancy and eternity) which are in their turn balanced and controlled by their 'love' counterparts (omnipresence, omnipotence and glory). What this enables Barth to do is, on the one hand, to give priority to what can be called the personal and biblical attributes, those, that is, primarily revealed in the economy of divine action as narrated in scripture – mercy, patience, and so on; but, on the other, to engage in their light, with the traditional treatment of the attributes by giving due account of the more metaphysical and philosophical terms, like eternity and omnipresence. That is to reverse the order found in so much of the history of the topic, where the a priori, abstract and impersonal – attributes deriving from the analogy of causality – provide a foundation – an essentially contradictory one, as it has turned out – for the personal.

Some brief examples will show how Barth's trinitarian dialectic shapes the doctrine. If we first refer to the classical definition of omnipotence, as found in Aquinas, and virtually a scholastic commonplace, we shall notice the difference: 'Therefore everything that does not imply a contradiction in terms, is numbered among those possible things in respect of which God is called omnipotent . . .'[10] Barth is wary of anything that might suggest a deification of power in itself – not that that is necessarily the implication of Aquinas' definition – and argues that it is necessary to begin rather where God's power is seen paradigmatically at

---

[9] Barth, *Church Dogmatics*, 2/1, pp. 353, 359.
[10] Aquinas, *Summa Theologiae*, 1. 25. 3.

work, in the cross of Jesus. 'Power in itself is not merely neutral. Power in itself is evil.'[11] That does two things: it grounds a conception of divine and ordered power in the biblical narrative; and it produces a conception of unlimited divine power which is controlled by the doctrine of the incarnation, which is an action, we must note. In a later volume, Barth picks up a saying of Gregory of Nyssa which makes a similar point, that the Son's 'descent to humility which took place in the incarnation of the Word is not only not excluded by the divine nature but signifies its greatest glory: περιουσία τίς ἐστιν τῆς δυνάμεως [an overflow of power]'.[12] He realizes that trinitarian control is necessary:

> Already in the creed the *omnipotentem* is not to be separated from the *Deum patrem* nor is the latter to be explained by the former. The omnipotence of which the creed speaks is the omnipotence of God the Father, the omnipotence of the God and Father who reveals Himself to be God and Father in accordance with the remaining content of the creed, and is therefore of one essence with the Son and the Holy Spirit.[13]

Similarly revealing is the treatment of immutability, aspects of which we have already met in Chapter 4, and which Barth seeks to personalize and moralize, preferring to speak of the divine constancy. Rejecting one treatment of this attribute in the Protestant scholastics, according to which God is the pure *immobile*, he comments:

> [W]e must not make any mistake: the pure *immobile* is –

[11] Barth, *Church Dogmatics*, 2/1, p. 524.
[12] Barth, *Church Dogmatics*, 4/1, p. 192, citing Gregory of Nyssa, *Or. Cat.* 24.
[13] Barth, *Church Dogmatics*, 2/1, p. 524.

death. If, then, the pure *immobile* is God, death is God. That is, death is posited as absolute and explained as the first and last and only real.[14]

The spelling out of Barth's concept is made by appeal to the continuity of God's action in creation, reconciliation and redemption.

> [I]t is by the incarnation that God has revealed His truly immutable being as free love in the perfection in which, on the basis of the incarnation, we recognise it again and find it confirmed in His acts as Creator, Reconciler and Redeemer. God is 'immutably' the One whose reality is seen in His condescension in Jesus Christ, in His self-offering and self-concealment . . .[15]

Characteristically, these developments, though founded in the Trinity, are largely christological in orientation, and it is in the last words of the latter citation, 'self-offering and self-concealment', that we shall find the key both to the structure of Barth's treatment of the attributes and to its chief weakness.

The structure of Barth's discussion of the attributes corresponds precisely with that of the doctrine of the Trinity in the previous volume of the *Church Dogmatics*. There, the dialectic is of revelation and hiddenness, the former expressing God's making himself known in the world, the latter the freedom of his self-revelation in time. The

[14] Barth, *Church Dogmatics*, 2/1, p. 494.
[15] Barth, *Church Dogmatics*, 2/1, p. 517. Jaroslav Pelikan, *The Christian Tradition. A History of the Development of Doctrine* (5 volumes, Chicago and London: Chicago University Press, 1971–1989), vol. 1, p. 22 states that in Judaism 'the immutability of God was seen as the trustworthiness of his covenanted relation to his people in the concrete history of his judgement and mercy, rather than as a primarily ontological category'. I owe this reference to Demetrios Bathrellos.

programmatic statement, 'Revelation in the Bible means the self-unveiling, imparted to men, of the God who cannot be unveiled to men', though thrice repeated, is fundamentally twofold in structure, with the weight thrown on the contrast of 'self-unveiling' and 'cannot be unveiled'. Corresponding to the Son's revelation is the Father's hiddenness and freedom. '[E]ven in the form He assumes when He reveals Himself God is free to reveal Himself or not to reveal Himself. . . . God's self-unveiling remains an act of sovereign divine freedom.'[16] This is clearly a reference to the fatherhood of God: 'God's fatherhood, too, is God's Lordship in His revelation.'[17]

In sum, the polarity of love and freedom in the doctrine of the divine perfections corresponds to the Son–Father duality in the preceding volume. That it is in a twofold pattern that Barth takes up the theme of the divine perfections is therefore not an accident and suggests that the doctrine of the Spirit is not determinative for the treatment of the attributes. That raises a question. What might happen to our topic if we were to introduce a more explicitly pneumatological element? The Holy Spirit is the perfecting Spirit, breaking in from the eschaton to perfect first the humanity of Jesus and through him that of those for whom he died. What implications might it have for our understanding of the being of God that he is Spirit as well as Father and Son? John Zizioulas has famously argued that God's being is communion. Communion, too, is an eschatological reality, because all true human communion with God and between human beings is an anticipation of the fellowship of the life to come. May we say – taking up once again the hint supplied by Basil – that the Spirit perfects the

16 Barth, *Church Dogmatics*, I/1, p. 321.
17 Barth, *Church Dogmatics*, I/1, p. 324.

life of the eternal Trinity by so relating the Father and Son that together the three are one being in communion?[18] In that case, how might our understanding of the one who *makes perfect* affect our doctrine of the divine *perfections*? Let us try to think fully trinitarianly about one contentious attribute, before moving in the next chapter to say something about the doctrine of God in more detail.

II *The Freedom of God*

We have seen that a dialectic of revealedness and love, on the one hand, and of hiddenness and freedom, on the other, are central to the shaping of Barth's doctrine of God. The question must be whether this leads to an over-voluntarist understanding of freedom; that is, one oriented to absolute rather than ordered freedom. The reason is something like this. We do need a doctrine of the absolute freedom of God, in the respect that God's actions are not necessary: he does not have to create a world, nor, having done it, to perfect it. It follows that the being of the creation as creation and not as the outflow of God's being is what gives it its own distinct reality, and this distinct particularity of the creation as creation derives from God's freely making it what it is. The doctrine of the Trinity is essential to the maintenance of such a teaching, showing that God is both self-sufficient in himself – the doctrine of the divine *aseity* – and creates and remains in relationship with the world that is other than he. Thus we do need a doctrine of divine freedom which corres-

[18] That would be a version, though a rather different one, of Augustine's conception of the Spirit as the bond of love between the Father and the Son. In this case, the Spirit is not the bond but the agent (mediator?) of love as a third person, a hypostasis with his own particular being.

ponds to what we might consider to be a 'natural' understanding of freedom: God creates, but is not bound to.

However, without a fully trinitarian construal of the
divine freedom, we shall be in danger of being left with a
mere voluntarism, a *potentia absoluta* which appears to
give God no reason to create except sheer arbitrariness. On
such an account, he creates by sheer will, and not by a will
formed by love. We shall also break the analogy between
divine and human freedom, or, perhaps better, in Scotist
terms, the elements of univocity in the uses of the word
freedom of God and of ourselves that enable us to understand both God and ourselves more satisfactorily. Let us
pause to consider the matter of freedom. In relation to
God, human freedom comes from the divine action that
graciously creates, upholds and redeems the creature who
has preferred slavery to freedom. To be free is to be set free
by the Spirit of the Father who is the Spirit of freedom. That
is to say, true freedom is realized in communion with God,
for unfreedom is, essentially, the loss of a right relationship
to God. In terms of the way that freedom which is given
works itself out in the world, we must say that freedom is
a function of communion at the human level also. Our
freedom is what we each make of our own particularity,
and none of us are truly the particular persons we are
created to be except in love and fellowship with our neighbour. In sum, both freedom and its loss are a function of
our relation to the other, and especially the divine other,
the creator. To be out of true communion is to be unfree; to
be free is to be for and with the other, both the divine and
the human other. Accordingly, freedom is never absolute,
but always structured and ordered, either wrongly or
rightly – as a matter of fact, always, this side of eternity, a
combination of both.

In what sense may we speak of an ordered or structured freedom both within God's being and in his relations *ad extra*? What reason, for example, might there be, other than sheer arbitrary will, for God's creation of the world? Might there be something within his eternal being which grounds what he does? John Zizioulas has located the basis of all God is and does in the person of the Father, who freely, though timelessly, begets the Son and breathes the Spirit, thus constituting an eternal communion which is the source of created communion.[19] While there is much to be said for the Cappadocian teaching that the Father is the source of both the being and the divinity of the other two persons, there must be some doubt about the rather voluntarist terms in which this freedom is expressed. A more pneumatologically structured concept of freedom might mitigate such a tendency. If the Spirit is sent by the Father through the Son to perfect the creation, what place might he be conceived to have in structuring the being of the triune God, and particularly the freedom of the godhead? Robert Jenson has made an attempt to do this, basing his argument on that of Luther's *De servo Arbitrio*. 'God is freedom antecedent to himself as determinate free will. He can intelligibly be said to be this as the Father is the source of the Son and both are freed in the Spirit. God is rapt by another without dependence on an other than God.'[20] Similarly, he suggests that 'the Spirit liberates God the Father from himself, to be in fact fatherly, to be the actual *arche* of deity; and so is indeed otherwise originated from

[19] John D. Zizioulas, *Being as Communion. Studies in Personhood and the Church* (London: Darton, Longman and Todd, 1985), pp. 87–9, but, in a sense, *passim*.

[20] Robert W. Jenson, 'An Ontology of Freedom in the *De Servo Arbitrio* of Luther', *Modern Theology* 10 (1994), 247–52 (250).

that source than is the Son'.[21] If the only freedom for creatures is freedom that is given, freedom for and with the
other (God first and then the creaturely other); if freedom is
only freedom in relation, might not the same be true of
God? Economically speaking, God's free creation is free
because it is ordered through the Son and perfected by the
Spirit. Similarly, his gracious reconciliation is free because
it is achieved by the Son through the Spirit's perfecting of
his free life of obedience. What might this mean for the
eternal Trinity? May we say that the triune life is free by
virtue of the free but ordered perichoresis – the τάξις – of
Father, Son and Spirit in which there is constituted a communion in which each of the hypostases is what he is from
and through the others? Thus, whether or not we put it
precisely in the way that Jenson does, we might say that
divine freedom is that which consists at once in the Father's
breathing of the Spirit through the Son, and the Spirit's
reciprocal perfecting of the love which God is through the
Son. On such an account, freedom is indeed a function of
that holy love, of that love which is the essence of God.

That leads us into a concluding point about the nature of
freedom. If freedom is like love, indeed, a function of love,
then it is not an absolute possession, an attribute construed
a priori. Let us instead return to the brief discussion of the
will in Chapter 2. There it was suggested that the will is not
a thing, a hypostasis, but refers to a mode of action of a
person-in-relation. So it is with God: freedom is a mode of
personal action. In that case, God's freedom is a form of
unconstrained and yet determined action which is determined because personally shaped by the relations of Father,

---

[21] Robert W. Jenson, *Systematic Theology*, volume 1, *The Triune
God*; volume 2, *The Works of God* (New York and Oxford: Oxford
University Press, 1997, 1999), vol. 1, p. 158.

Son and Spirit, and yet unconstrained because it is a form of love. Perhaps we have now reached a stage when we should not attempt to speculate any further, but make a point which will take us into the next phase of discussion. Is freedom an attribute or a form or mode of God's action? Indeed, what kind of distinction should we draw between the two? We have seen that attribute is best understood in terms of action, in God's case the action in which God is who he is. In the next chapter, we shall seek to explore something of what it might mean for the doctrine of the attributes if we follow up the two trinitarian 'definitions' of God to be found in scripture, that he is spirit and that he is love.

7

Attribute and Action

I *The Knowledge of God*

The church's theologians and philosophers have not necessarily been wrong in the lists of attributes they have, over the centuries, assembled. What have often been wrong are, first, the way in which they have understood them and, second, the way they have, often by the order of treatment, weighted them wrongly, emphasizing in particular the negative over against the positive, the cosmological and timeless against the historical and temporal. It may be that there is a place for most or all of the traditional attributes, though it may be necessary to consider carefully the form of some of them, perhaps especially simplicity and impassibility. The latter will form the main case study we shall consider in this chapter. But first, an attempt to sum up the position we have reached so far.

God is interesting in and for himself. That is a slogan much loved by Eberhard Jüngel – repeated in a recent book – and it provides the principle for our discussion.[1] The worship and knowledge of God is not based on self-interest, or any other end, though other ends may be attained by it,

[1] Eberhard Jüngel, *Justification. The Heart of the Christian Faith. A Theological Study with an Ecumenical Purpose*, translated by Jeffrey F. Cayzer (Edinburgh and New York: T. & T. Clark, 2001), p. 54.

but is simply because God is who and what he is, to be wor-
shipped and glorified for ever. The celebration of God's
being is just that. So Barth begins his treatment of the divine
attributes: 'God is. This is the simple statement which we
have to develop and explain . . .'[2] As we have seen, the
Bible, and especially the New Testament, is for christological reasons insistent that God is knowable because he is
known. In Jesus, and in those anticipations of the incarnation we meet in the Old Testament, God communicates
something of himself: he gives himself in his Son. This in
its turn generates two subsidiary principles. The first is
christological: 'God gives himself, but he does not give
himself away.'[3] God does not empty himself into the world,
but relates to it while retaining his integrity as God and his
distinction from the world. The second subsidiary principle
is pneumatological. God is known by us when and in so far
as he himself wills. This applies to all forms of the knowledge of God, even – especially – to that which is claimed to
be possible through what is called natural revelation. In the
light of human sin and blindness, the Spirit has to dispel our
ignorance, so that we may see what is there.

This principle that God is trinitarianly knowable is one
which is most neglected in the tradition, and, indeed, may
raise the question of whether we need one traditional attribute, that of the unknowability of God, at all. It undoubtedly
calls into question the way the matter has often been put in
both East and West. In the East, the official doctrine,
associated especially with Gregory Palamas, is that we do
not know the being or essence of God, but know him
through his energies. In the West, certainly until the late
medievals – beginning, as we have seen, with Scotus – and

[2] Karl Barth, *Church Dogmatics*, translation edited by G. W. Bromiley
and T. F. Torrance (Edinburgh: T. & T. Clark, 1957–1975), 2/1, p. 257.
[3] Barth, *Church Dogmatics*, 4/1, p. 185.

the Reformers began their critique, the doctrine was the Neoplatonically formed teaching that we do not know God in himself, but from his effects. It seems to me that both of these ways of putting it are at best misleading, and that in the light of the gospel we must be free to confess that we are granted to know the very being of God.

Therefore what may seem, in the light of much of the Christian tradition, to be an outrageous claim must be made: that it is part of the Christian claim to truth that human beings are given to know the being of God. To be sure, there are two senses in which knowledge of the divine essence is excluded. (1) One cannot have a full rational account of or define finally in conceptual terms what it is for God to be God. Indeed, it is part of the burden of the first three chapters to claim that a deep-seated weakness of the tradition is its claim too confidently to know too much, particularly of the negative attributes, and that this is not as paradoxical as it might appear. In this regard at least – in this regard only – a version of the doctrine of God's unknowability is essential. Although God is objectively knowable, he sets the conditions of and limits to human knowledge of himself. (2) Nor can one have, so to speak, an inside view of the being of God, to know God by direct vision; that, according to part of the Christian tradition, is reserved for the kingdom of heaven, when the blessed will be granted the beatific vision.[4] God is incomprehensible in

---

[4] That way of putting the matter is in any case deeply flawed, suggesting as it does a mediated knowledge as a defective form of vision in the present, an immediate one at the end. At issue is the *form* of mediation with which we are concerned. Commenting on Aquinas' eschatology, Robert C. Doyle remarks that 'God is indeed wonderful, but the "final vision" of him is not static (an intellectual relationship between "substances"); it is relational (between persons) and mutual . . .' *Eschatology and the Shape of Christian Belief* (Carlisle: Paternoster Press, 1999), p. 143.

not being graspable; but not incomprehensible in the sense
of being entirely beyond our understanding. He can and
does give himself to be conceived by us. 'In His essence, as
it is turned to us in His activity, He is so constituted that He
can be known by us.'[5]

In order to move to an account of what we can know, let
me begin by revising the two slogans. 'We know God only
by his effects': yes, if by 'effect' is meant not a cosmologically abstracted first cause, but the *actions* of God – creation,
redemption, etc. – towards and in the created world; God
not abstracted from matter, but involved in it. We know
the divine energies: yes, but only if energies refer not to
something midway between the world and the divine
persons but to the action of the Holy Spirit.[6] Thus
Colossians 2.12 speaks of : 'the *energeias* of him who raised
Jesus Christ from the dead', while Ephesians 1.19f., literally
translated, reads, 'through the *energeian* of the strength of
his might which he exercised (*energeken*) in Christ, raising
him from the dead . . .'. Unless they are glossed in this way,
the traditional slogans effectively deny the mediatorial
work of the Son and the Spirit in making the Father known.
But if we *know* the hypostases – by the mediation of scripture and the church's life and proclamation – then we know
the *substance*, being, essence, *Wesen*, etc., of God, for there
is nothing else to be known. The three persons *are* the being
of God, and if we know the Father through the Son and in
the Spirit we know the being of God.

To repeat, this does not imply that we have an 'inside'
sight, or an exhaustive knowledge; indeed, it is not a matter

---

[5] Barth, *Church Dogmatics*, 2/1, p. 65.

[6] Thomas Binney's great hymn brings out the action of the two hands
of the Father in salvation: 'an offering and a sacrifice, a holy Spirit's
energies, an advocate with God'. 'Eternal Light', in *Rejoice and Sing*
(Oxford: Oxford University Press, 1991), no. 83.

of sight or of that kind of knowledge at all. Rather, knowledge is a form of personal relation, a version of the notion
of knowledge by acquaintance. Nor is there a claim that
our words as they stand begin to be adequate to the task,
but the Spirit makes them adequate, as and in so far as God
pleases, and if the Fourth Gospel, to mention but one, is
right, God has so pleased and continues to do so.[7] In sum
God's being is known in and through his action, his triune
act. God's action is triune in the sense that it is the action of
Father, Son and Spirit, whose *opera ad extra* are inseparable from one another, though they are distributed, so to
speak, between the three persons: the Father being the
originating source of action, which he performs through
the Son's involvement in the created world and the Spirit's
perfecting of created things in anticipation of and on the
Last Day. To repeat from a previous chapter the patristic
formula: all divine action, and that includes the actions in
which human beings are granted a measure, appropriate to
their condition, begins with the Father, takes shape through
the Son and reaches its completion in the Spirit.

II Beginning with John

There are two apparent definitions, both of them to be found
in the Johannine literature, of the God who is known in this
way. The first is that taken up by Charnock at the outset of
his treatment of the divine attributes: 'God is Spirit'. As we
have seen, the tendency of the tradition is to discover the
meaning of this abstractly, by various reflections on the

---

[7] Recall the point made by Jüngel in connection with Barth about the
gain to language involved in the act of predicating attributes of God.
Above, p. 74.

claim that God is not material. It is a largely negative abstraction from supposed features of the created world, and we are reminded of Gregory's warning against the one 'who states what God is not without going on to say what He is'. There is no need to deny that this is indeed the case, but it is not the whole of it. It is part of the human condition that we are a different kind of being from God: 'the Egyptians are men and not God, their horses flesh and not spirit' (Isa. 31.3). And yet two further general points have to be added and they make all the difference. The first is that whatever may be the particular point made about the Egyptians, it is also the case that God gives human beings a share in that elusive reality called spirit.[8] It is their particular blessing and endowment that they are created open to God in a way other creatures are not. Other creatures are given life, but only into Adam does God breathe the *ruach* of life. In so far as human beings are open to God, it is not primarily because they are rational beings but because they are persons: like God in being, so far and so long as God grants – for he gives and takes away our spirit (Ps. 104) – open to God and to the other. That is one of the implications of the doctrine of the image of God, and it is amplified if we refer to a crucial aspect of this for the New Testament, and especially for Paul, that the distinction between flesh and spirit is not dualistic but eschatological. Paul's contrast between flesh and spirit is not between matter and mind but between the old, fallen humanity of Adam and the new humanity in Christ. 'Flesh' refers to fallen humanity; 'spirit' to the redeemed, eschatological humanity which has already taken shape in Christ and begins, through the

---

[8] Hans Walter Wolff, *Anthropology of the Old Testament*, translated by Margaret Kohl (London: SCM Press, 1974), ch. 4: 'Man as he is Empowered'.

Spirit, to take place in those who are being conformed to his image, when and as God pleases. In sum, to have spirit means to be open to God's creative and redemptive Spirit. Spirit is thus a communicable attribute.

The second point gives us the reason why this is so and shows us its basis. That God is spirit, generally, does not mean simply that he is not material but that he is able to encompass both what we call spirit and what we call matter. To *have* spirit is to be open to the other – God, the human other and the world; to *be* spirit, as God is, is to be able to cross the boundary between creator and creature, even to the extent of God the Son's becoming identical with Jesus of Nazareth by the power of the Spirit. In scripture, God's being spirit appears to refer to the capacity of the creator to cross ontological boundaries: to interact with and become part of that which he is not. It is to do with creative and redemptive power. Such a definition is implicitly trinitarian, but that is not adequate on its own, as the example of Hegel shows. God is spirit for Hegel, but spirit which becomes not only related to but ultimately identical with the human rational spirit. The created world is not assumed and redeemed, but idealized and dematerialized. We must therefore go further and seek a more concrete and incarnational construal of the text. The doctrine of the Trinity must be grounded in the Word made truly flesh. What does the Gospel of John suggest by glossing his definition, 'and those who worship him must worship him in spirit and in truth'? The expression comes in the course of an argument about the Temple and its (Samaritan) altern-ative, and so is about worship as active approach to the presence of God. It presents an account of the mediation of God's presence and human response to it. And so the construal must not only be trinitarian, but contain an explicitly christological reference. 'In spirit and in truth' means in the Holy Spirit and in him who is, according to this Gospel, the truth, Jesus of Nazareth, the Word made flesh. God's being spirit is, at the level of the economy, God self-defined in this particular free self-identification with part of the created order for the sake of the remainder of it. The specification of God's difference from the world – that God is entirely Spirit – can be understood only in the light of God's free relation to the world. We shall have to pursue this further, but only after other things have been said.

The second place where something like a definition of God is given is the First Letter of John, chapter 4. The context is the author's elaborations of the love of the Christian community and his claim that there is a close relation between knowledge of God and love of the neighbour, and then also between those and a knowledge of who God is. 'Whoever does not love does not know God, because God is love' (v. 8). This love is clearly something that God is, in himself, so that to be known it had to be revealed in the world, to move outside itself into relation with another. The implication of verse 12 ('No one has ever seen God, but if we love one another, God lives in us . . . ') is that we know God even though no one has ever seen him, and we must here refer also to John 1.18: 'no one has ever seen God . . . his only Son has made him known'. The important point for us is that John's theology of the *economy* of love – for it is that with which he is concerned – is grounded in a conception of God's *being* as love. The love that God is is realized in time (1) christologically (1 John 4.9: 'This is how God showed his love among us: He he sent his one and only Son into the world'; v. 14: 'the Father has sent his Son to be the saviour of the world'); and (2) pneumatologically (v. 2: 'Every spirit that acknowledges that Jesus Christ has come in the flesh is from God'; v. 13: 'We know that we live in him and he in us, because he has given us of his Spirit'). In the economy, that God is love is demonstrated by the three-fold shape of his loving agency.

At this stage, we have to take a crucial step which will lead us into other aspects of the doctrine of the divine attributes. The fact that this love takes the form of God's sending his Son to be a sacrifice for our sins (ἱλασμὸν) (v. 10) shows us the form that this love takes. Here we are well advised to prefer Forsyth's stress on the holiness of this love to that of Barth on its freedom. God's love is indeed free, but its holiness encompasses far more adequately the shape of the love as involving the overcoming of the sin that brings men and women into enmity with God. Charnock's magnificent expression of this makes the point:

> Without it [holiness], his patience would be an indulgence to sin, his mercy a fondness, his wrath a madness, his power a tyranny, his wisdom an unworthy subtlety. It is this gives a decorum to all. . . . In acts of man's vindictive justice there is something of impurity, perturbation, passion, some mixture of cruelty; but none of these fall upon God in the severest acts of wrath.[9]

In the holiness of God is encompassed a range of concepts which spell out the kind of God with whom we are to do: otherness from the world as its creator, purity as its redeemer and judge, holiness as the consistency between God's being and his action.[10] If we focus our attention on the christological dimensions, we shall say with Forsyth

---

[9] Stephen Charnock, *The Existence and Attributes of God* (Grand Rapids: Baker, 2000), vol. 2, pp. 113–14.
[10] I owe this point to Rufus Burton.

that God's holy love is demonstrated on the cross, which marks the centre of God's rejection of sin and redemption of the sinner. Because God is holy, his action encompasses both of these apparent contraries. Pneumatologically speaking, there are things to add. The Spirit is the one who makes holy. This means that by bringing the sinner to the Father through the ascended Christ the Spirit perfects by making holy that which had unfitted itself to come into God's presence. The Spirit's work is the eschatological work of perfecting through the redemption won by Christ that which was created and fell from its proper being. It is this connection with perfecting that above all characterizes the holiness of the Spirit.

A discussion of holy love in action leads naturally into the attributes which a reading of scripture would bring first to mind: mercy, wrath, grace, covenant-love (a feature of which is God's calling of Israel to be his holy people). Reading, for example, the opening chapters of Genesis will demonstrate these attributes in action. God's relation to the world begins with the utterly sovereign work of creation, and upon it supervenes, as sin disrupts creation's movement to perfection, the judgment of Adam and Eve, and, indeed, the promise of redemption in the eschatological judgment of their tempter; the merciful punishment of Cain, limited as it is by the mark set upon the criminal so that he shall undergo no further punishment; the holy wrath at the human sin of men which triggers the flood and the covenant mercy beyond and supervening upon it. All this is marked by God's patience – interestingly a word formed from the same root as impassibility – which is incomparably defined by Barth:

We define God's patience as His will, deep-rooted in His essence and constituting His divine being and action, to

allow to another . . . space and time for the development
of its own existence, thus conceding to this existence a
reality side by side with His own, and fulfilling His will
towards this other in such a way that He does not
suspend and destroy it as this other but accompanies and
sustains and allows it to develop in freedom.[11]

These are all, it must be noted, attributes in action. They
reveal certain forms of action as an expression in time of
the eternal being of God who, as we have already seen, is
different in kind from the gods of the nations, with their
pettiness and the limitations on their power. All of these
forms of action come together in the career of Jesus, who is
God's sovereignty, mercy, justice, love, patience and holiness in action. Schematically, and therefore over-simply,
we might say that God's power is revealed in the victory
of the cross and resurrection, his justice in the overcoming and therefore re-establishing of the law on the basis
of grace, his patience in giving the wicked time and oppor-
tunity to repent, and his holiness in the purity and perfection of the sacrificial self-offering that is the whole
ministry and its completion in the cross, resurrection and
ascension.

If, then, it is true that God's action reveals his being; if
through the acts we are given to know the actor, what have
we to say about the eternal being of God, the attributes
which make him what he is essentially? We can approach
an answer with another question. How do we link the two
Johannine definitions of God? God is holy love because he
is spirit in a quite definite way. His is a love that is 'complete'
because of the unbroken communion that is the perichoresis
of the Father, Son and Spirit. The Father begets the Son

[11] Barth, *Church Dogmatics*, 2/1, pp. 409–10.

as his other in an eternal act of pure love – agapeistic in orienting itself entirely to the other – while the Spirit is sent to complete 'the divine and blessed Trinity'.[12] Robert Jenson is similar. The Spirit 'is another who in his own intention liberates Father and Son to love each other'.[13] Might we say further that the Spirit relates the Father and the Son – not as 'love' but as the *energy* of their love, thus guaranteeing their integrity in their distinctness? The need here is to avoid the western tendency to conceive the Spirit as the one who closes the circle of the divine love, replacing it with an orientation outwards, so that corresponding to the Spirit's constitution of the otherness in relation of the Father and Son in the eternal Trinity is an orientation to the other which is the created world. This is a way of maintaining the direction outwards of *agape* (see again 1 John 4. 10, for the basis of our knowledge that God is love being the fact that he sent his Son as an atoning sacrifice).[14] The Son, we might say, is the principle of the Father's movement into relation with the other, the Spirit its motive power. Just as economically God's holiness is the consistency of his act with his being, to give an adequate account of the immanent Trinity we must bring into play more than has usually been done the eschatological function of the Spirit. There would appear to be two focuses: the orientation to otherness and the perfection of particularity. First, by perfecting the communion of the Trinity, the Spirit is the Spirit of holiness, first in God himself and then in the world. In the immanent Trinity, for God to be holy is for

[12] Basil, *Hex.* 2. 6. The word translated 'to complete' is συμπληρωτικόν.

[13] Robert W. Jenson, *Systematic Theology*, volume 1, *The Triune God*; volume 2, *The Works of God* (New York and Oxford: Oxford University Press, 1997, 1999), vol. 1, p. 156.

[14] 'Not that we loved God, but that he loved us, and sent his Son . . .'

God to be perfect, which includes notions of completeness and communion. Holiness therefore is God's eternal perfection, the perfection of personal love in relation, a perfection which takes shape in all of God's acts *ad extra*. And second, the perfection of particularity is achieved because the Father, Son and Spirit are constitutive of one another as particularly what they are, distinct persons who are what they are from and for the other.

Such a theology gives us two complementary and utterly necessary outcomes: an account of God's utter self-sufficiency and his gracious orientation outwards, so that creator and creation are not opposites – as we saw in the third chapter, almost an axiom of the *via negativa* – but two realms which are positively related, and only become opposites by the sin and evil which set themselves in opposition to God's goodness. If, then, we consider the being of God as creator in relation to his creation, the aspect of God's holy love with which we are concerned is denoted by the attribute of aseity, that God has his being entirely in and from himself. This is, however, to be construed positively, not negatively as sometimes appears to be the case.[15] If the Son and the Spirit are in different ways focuses of God's movement outwards, to the other, God's aseity, the doctrine of his ontological integrity and completeness, will serve as the basis both of the creation's integrity, as truly itself by virtue of its being created in the Son and by the power of the Spirit, and of the utter gratuity and sovereignty of God's atoning love in Christ.

The mention of the Spirit's eschatological work of perfecting belongs here: that the one 'who completes the divine and blessed Trinity' is the vehicle through the Son of at once the divine communion and the perfecting, through

[15] See above, Chapter 2, p. 20 for Barth's point about this.

redemption, of the creation. Linked with aseity must be simplicity, which again must be defined positively, not merely as absence of composition. The link with aseity is made by a definition suggested by Steve Holmes: 'To describe God as "simple" means that God is ontologically basic.'[16] Much traditional argument tends to take the form that, just as material things are constituted of parts, which can be separated, so God is 'without body, passion or parts'. That, again, conceives God and the creation in terms of opposing attributes: material things have parts; God, by a process of negation, is supposed to be simple. There is, however, a positive way of construing simplicity if we think in terms of perichoresis, of the relations of persons. The Father, Son and Spirit constitute one God without remainder because their communion is perfect and unbroken. The being of Father, Son and Spirit is constituted entirely from being who they particularly are in their relations one to another.[17] The Trinity is indeed not constituted of parts – which can be separated – but of persons, who are distinguishable but not separable, and therefore constitute a 'simple' God. So long as the doctrine of simplicity is a function of the doctrine of God's triune and holy love, we may affirm it gladly; indeed, it is an essential part of the argument that 'There are not Three Gods.'[18]

A definition sometimes offered of divine simplicity is its requirement that any one attribute is essentially the same as

[16] Stephen R. Holmes, '"Something Much Too Plain to Say": Towards a Defence of the Doctrine of Divine Simplicity', *Neue Zeitschrift für Systematische Theologie und Religionsphilosophie* 43 (2001), 139.

[17] For examples of trinitarian defences of divine simplicity, see Holmes, 'Something Much Too Plain to Say', 147–9.

[18] 'Gregory of Nyssa's *Concerning We Should Think of Saying That There Are Not Three Gods* to Ablabius', in W. G. Rusch, editor, *The Trinitarian Controversy* (Philadelphia: Fortress Press, 1980), pp. 149–61.

others. As it stands, that will not do, in danger as it is of a merely nominalist construal: that it may seem to us that there is a variety of attributes, but that is really only from our perspective. We must listen again to Barth's warning about the kind of unity with which we are concerned: that 'the very unity of [God's] being consists in the multiplicity, individuality and diversity of His perfections . . .'[19] If we are to heed the variety of revelation, so we must find room for a multiplicity of divine ways of acting. Though God's wrath is a function of his holy love, it is not identical with it, at least in the respect that it is the form holiness takes with respect to sin and evil. The point of the doctrine of divine simplicity is rather that the attributes must be defined from and through one another as a function of the trinitarian perichoresis. To take what may appear to be an over-simple example, if we are to escape a concept of justice according to which God merely punishes evil and rewards good, we must construe God's justice christologically as that form of action by which he overcomes evil by undergoing its consequences in Jesus; and pneumatologically as that by which through the Spirit he makes the cross and resurrection the basis and guarantee of the eschatological defeat of evil.

In the light of all this, what are we to make of the distinction, which was important for the Reformation tradition, between communicable and incommunicable attributes: between those, to repeat an earlier simplification, that God keeps to himself and those he spreads around? Speaking of Jüngel on justification, John Webster writes that, 'divine righteousness is not an incommunicable attribute of God (equivalent to divine eternity or omniscience, for example)

---

[19] Barth, *Church Dogmatics*, 2/1, p. 332.

but is rather to be identified with God's action in declaring and making sinners righteous'.[20] As we have also seen, God makes holy but he does not make omnipotent; God is *a se*, while the world's being is dependent on that of its creator. If, however, attributes are revealed in action, the following principle should apply: that the incommunicable attributes, in so far as there are any, are there for the sake of the communicable. God's orientation, as we have seen, is to the other, both in himself and *ad extra*. On such an understanding, the incommunicable form the basis for the communicable. There are, therefore, no attributes which are strictly and completely incommunicable. (Contrast this with the citation early in Chapter 2 above from Johannes Braun, where he makes the opposite point, that all the attributes are primarily incommunicable: a God *incurvatus in se*. 'Strictly speaking none are communicable, since they are *proprietates* (God's very own).'[21]) God does not make omnipotent, but through his Spirit he does communicate power; he does not make a creation that exists from itself, but he does create one that has its being in itself, albeit being that is given to it:

> so the work of God is that which God works in us, the virtue of God, by which he makes us powerful, the wisdom of God by which he makes us wise, the strength of God, the salvation of God, the glory of God . . . [22]

---

[20] John Webster, 'Introduction' to Jüngel, *Justification*, p. ix.

[21] See above, p. 33–4.

[22] 'ut opus Dei, id est, quod operatur in nobis Deus, virtus Dei, qua nos potentes facit, sapientia Dei, qua nos sapientes facit, fortitudo Dei, salus Dei, gloria Dei.' Luther, WA 54, 186, 11–13. Cited by Christoph Schwöbel, 'Die "Botschaft der Versöhnung" (2 Kor 5,19) und die Versöhnungslehre', *Biblischer Text und theologische Theoriebildung*, edited by S. Chapman and others (Neukirchen, 2001), p. 165.

Moreover, if the order of our treatment has been right, it is the communicable attributes which are the focus through which the others, especially love, holiness and spirit, are to be construed.[23] In the order of knowing we move from the communicable to the incommunicable – rather than from some a priori considerations about what 'God' means; while in the order of being, things move in the reverse direction, because God's action flows from what he truly is in eternity.

III A Case Study: Impassibility

We have met already some discussion of the attribute of impassibility: the doctrine that God cannot suffer. We have seen that it is important as part of the early Christian polemic against anthropomorphism. God is not envious, nor swayed by any of the passions that affect our judgment and action. But, as we have also seen, such an argument can cut both ways, and prevent us attributing to God compassion and other forms of action which appear to be intrinsic to a full biblical account of his action. As the long history of its discussion shows, it is a doctrine that damages as well as supports the gospel, for it undoubtedly served as one of the motive forces behind Nestorianism, which divided the person of Christ in order to preserve the eternal Son from the taint of suffering. (Divine impassibility provides support for Arianism also.)[24] In christology, the solution for

[23] Rufus Burton, research paper, King's College, London. '. . . the holiness of God is what makes any of the attributes of God communicable. Indeed, it is the important attributes that are communicable, holiness, love etc. We don't really need to be omni-anything to lead lives that glorify and enjoy God.'

[24] Werner Elert, *Der Ausgang der altkirchlichen Christologie* (Berlin: Lutherisches Verlagshaus, 1957).

the Fathers was something as follows. The Son cannot suffer in respect of his ontological integrity: he must remain fully God, unchangeably so; or how can we rely on the fact that this is truly divine salvation? The incarnation and cross are not events happening to God, but God victoriously achieving the defeat of evil. And yet as incarnate, as bearing the flesh of Adam and Eve, the Son can and does suffer death on the cross. It does, however, appear problematic to take this to mean, as we earlier read Anselm taking it, that God is compassionate towards us, but not truly in himself; that is to commit, or so it seems, another breach between act and being which derives from the uncomfortable coupling of the Greek and the Hebrew ways of construing God's aseity. If the Son suffers as incarnate, there must be a sense in which God suffers.

Yet we do need a version of the traditional doctrine in defence of God's sovereignty – or omnipotence, if we wish to use the traditional term. God is not at the mercy of either emotions or events in the created world. If the cross is a passion in that sense, there is no guarantee that it is sovereign divine action, and it may be made to appear that history will decide its outcome, rather than the sovereign power of God. Moltmann's repeated speaking of the grief of the Father risks rendering the Father passive.[25] Rather, the cross is the passion of the Son, but *as such* and in complete unity with it the omnipotent redemptive action of the Father. It is, to use Paul's characterization, the power and wisdom of God. It is the power of God in action because it is the means by which God meets evil on its own ground and defeats it without using its methods; it is divine wisdom

[25] Jürgen Moltmann, *The Crucified God. The Cross of Christ as the Foundation and Criticism of Christian Theology*, translated by R. A. Wilson and John Bowden (London: SCM Press, 1974), ch. 6.

in action because it is the only exercise of power that is proportionate to the need and condition of the sinner and successful in bringing about its end.

Such a way of stating the situation – the passion of the Son, but *as such* and in complete unity with it the redemptive action of the Father – appears to risk imperilling the unity of the divine act. Against that, again with the help of John's Gospel, it must be argued that the opposite is the case, that the Son's work is, as incarnate, to do the work of the Father, and only as he does it is he truly the Son. As has often been pointed out, Moltmann's account tends to introduce the division within God by making the so-called cry of dereliction not the climax of the Son's obedience but in some way a breach between God and God. We need here to maintain two trinitarian principles in harness. The first is that there is no separation between what the Father and the Son achieve; this is something not suffered so much as achieved through suffering. The second, equally important, principle is that there is at the same time a distinction between the acts of the Father and the Son. It is the particular calling of the Son to suffer, in obedience to the Father's will. He performs the work of God precisely by being the Son, the suffering servant. This in turn implies a distinction between the attributes of the Father and those of the Son. The Son is eternally the *incarnandus*, the one who is to be incarnate, is to identify himself with the flesh that he bore as Jesus of Nazareth. The Father as the one who wills this and brings it about by the power of his Spirit does it precisely by not suffering in that sense – because he does not bear fragile flesh – and so is impassibly sovereign and able to achieve what he wills *through* his Son's (substitutionary) suffering. In this context, Barth speaks of both command and obedience as being features of the eternal life of the Trinity, and while that may be to read too much of the economy into eternity, clearly implied is a *taxis* or order of superordination and subordination.[26]

Whatever else we do, we must not deprive the Son of his particular calling and function: to be sent to suffer on behalf of the world whose flesh he bears for that purpose. Yet do we not need, against the almost unanimous witness of the ancient church, to affirm that in a different respect from that of the Son, the Father also suffers? The Fathers rejected the doctrine known as patripassianism, that the Son's suffering is also the Father's, and for good reasons, because it was associated with Sabellianism, the teaching that God was successively Father, Son and Spirit (and so, it could seem, not truly any or all of them), and the church emerged with the teaching that 'one of the three has suffered in the flesh'.[27] Is this really necessary? It seems that here we reach the question of the distinctive being and action of the Son in relation to, to be sure, but in distinction from the Father. What is the nature of the distinction?

To answer that question we must ask another: what do we mean by 'suffering'? In the case of the Son, that is fairly clear: he actively allowed himself to be passively subject to the principalities and powers, but only as the mediator of the Father's act, indeed, as his own sovereign act also. He steadfastly set his face to go to Jerusalem (Luke 9.51); he lays down his life when and as he chooses (John 10.17–18). The Father's act is carried out by the active 'passion' of the Son: 'whose *passio* in history is as such *actio*'.[28] What then of the Father's suffering? Is there a difference between

---

[26] Barth, *Church Dogmatics*, 4/1, §59: 'The Obedience of the Son of God'.

[27] Elert, *Der Ausgang*, pp. 110–15.

[28] Barth, *Church Dogmatics*, 1/1, p. 144.

being swayed by emotion and accepting that, once there is a creation, God can be affected by its ill?[29] Such suffering as we speak of must come from within rather than being something imposed as foreign to the being of God. The Bible's God has a heart (Barth): the problem with the negative theology is that it tends to rule this out absolutely, and generate a metaphysically abstract doctrine of impassibility. Perhaps crucial is Paul's notion that the Father (sacrificially) gives up his Son to death, sending him to bear the consequences of human enmity with God. It is a mark of the Father's genuine compassion in action that (rather like Abraham in Genesis 22) he did not spare his only Son, the one on whom his loving purposes for the world depended, but gave him up for us all. In so far as it speaks of the Father's sacrifice, it is a kind of suffering. If perichoresis is true and is grounded in the economy of God's action, then in this act the Father must be seen both to command and to suffer his Son's total identification with man under judgment.

The notion of perichoresis also requires that we bring the doctrine of the Spirit to bear on our topic, because so far we have looked at this matter only in terms of the relation between Father and Son. What difference might the Spirit make? What does the sacrificial giving that leads to the sacrifice on the cross mean for the relationship of the Son to the Father mediated by the Spirit? Does it have to do with the perichoresis of Father, Son and Spirit worked out under the conditions of the Fall? The Son's relation to the Father remains as it should be – mediated by the Spirit – but not his

---

[29] See, again, God's reaction to wickedness in the story of Noah, Gen. 6.6, and, indeed, Hos. 11.8 also: 'My heart is changed within me . . .'.

relation to the world, which is distorted by sin and evil.[30] In support of such a contention there are the affirmations of the letter to the Hebrews that Jesus was made perfect through suffering and that he offered up his perfected life through the eternal Spirit. Suffering here has the meaning of 'what happened to him' through the whole course of his life and death, and has the connotations of endurance rather than passivity. The Spirit is the one who enables Jesus' suffering to be redemptive, to make it of *eschatological* significance, and therefore truly the Father's sovereign action.

That is to say, the suffering of the Son on the cross takes place only for the sake of the eschatological defeat of suffering. Suffering is what takes place in the created world as the result of the Fall: sin, sickness, the demonic are therefore those things that are to be overcome if the bondage of the creation to vanity is to be overcome. Apart from that, divine suffering will do little. To say to someone, 'I feel your pain' is not much of a help, unless it is a means to its overcoming. Indeed, simply to leave the matter with a statement that God shares our suffering runs the risk of affirming suffering, making it in some way the will of God. The point of the exercise, rather, is to remove suffering from the creation, not to affirm it or establish it as in some way a necessity for God or man. It is the opposition. This priority of redemption is undermined, if not actively subverted, by any breach of perichoresis; any suggestion that there is a rift in God. It seems therefore that the so-called cry of

[30] It is worth mentioning, but only as an aside, that one of the arguments used by Basil to establish the divinity of the person of the Spirit is that it is possible to grieve him (Basil, *On the Holy Spirit*, 19. 50). But we are not concerned here to give an account of the different ways in which Father, Son and Spirit might variously be supposed to suffer.

dereliction should not be seen in such terms, but as the final episode in the incarnate Son's total identification of himself, through the Spirit, with the lost human condition. Most simply, it is the cry of an Israelite expressing the self-distancing of that people from God as the result of their sin, the completion of Jesus' identification with Israel in his baptism.[31]

What is at stake in the doctrine of the impassibility of God? Undoubtedly, as we have already seen, what the doctrine expresses is the ontological integrity of God, his immunity from alteration in his being as the result of things done by creatures. It is linked with his moral consistency and integrity, as well as his sovereignty – the assurance that he cannot be deflected from achieving his purposes. This leads us to a positive account of immutability, one defined by historical action, as for example in Malachi 3.6: 'I the Lord do not change. So you, descendants of Jacob, are not destroyed.' Note that here, as in James 1.17 – 'who does not change, like shifting shadows' – the doctrine is linked with indefectibility of action, not with abstract ontological closedness. Once again, we meet an attribute made known in action rather than philosophical analysis. And yet there is a case for something of that, too. It has been suggested that part of the drive of the al Qa'eda campaign against America is a belief that if the holy places of their religion are violated, the being of their God is in some way threatened.[32] Against any such suggestion, we must insist that the God of Christian scripture can look after himself, and that

---

[31] 'A rabbi friend mentioned to me that Christians perceive Jesus' cry from the cross . . . as a profound moment of struggle between Father and Son; Jews, however, hear those words as the death cry of yet another Jewish victim.' Philip Yancey, *The Jesus I Never Knew* (London: Marshall Pickering, 1995), p. 50.

[32] I am grateful to Luke Bretherton for this example.

is why we know that he can look after the world. But that does not appear to prevent him from entering voluntarily into wrath against and sympathy for the erring creature. In particular, it cannot rule out what for many a Greek philosopher made Christianity incredible: the eternal and fully divine Son's taking flesh for the sake of the world. Here, for ancient and modern theology alike, the cross is literally the crux.

IV A Brief Conclusion

The opinion has already been cited in a footnote that the only really interesting attributes are the communicable ones, because that is the point of our doctrine of God: that men and women may become what they were created to be, those who are, because they are made in his image, *like* God. There are, however, as we have seen, a number of auxiliary attributes, which operate as that adjective suggests, to support the sovereignty and indefectibility of the divine action. The doctrine of the incommunicable attributes is rather like that of the immanent or eternal Trinity. Without them, God's power, grace and love would not be truly God's. Christoph Schwöbel makes the point in his defence of the immanent Trinity: 'How justified would we be in trusting the faithfulness of God's love if God were not eternally loving, but became a loving God when human beings reciprocate his love?'[33] So it is with impassibility, which – in the form I have attempted to expound it – far from being a denial of God's love serves in its support. It

[33] Christoph Schwöbel, 'God is Love: The Model of Love and the Trinity,' *Neue Zeitschrift für Systematische Theologie und Religionsphilosophie* 40 (1998), 322.

thus operates alongside aseity, simplicity, omnipotence and immutability. Aseity provides a necessary defence of God's ontological self-sufficiency; simplicity a defence of the indivisibility of his action, immutability of his utter constancy and consistency, impassibility of the indefectibility of his purposes for the perfection of his creation, and omnipotence of the guarantee that what God began in creation he will complete. Thus we end the chapter with versions of the ancient attributes, refined in the fire of God's action and of the doctrine that they are all in one respect at least essentially the same.

8

Hypostasis and Attribute

I *Three* Distinct *Triune Persons?*

Not only has there been a negative theology of the one God; there is a long tradition of a negative theology of the attributes of the three persons of the Trinity, including notably perhaps the oft-quoted patristic saying that the only difference of attribute between the Father and the Son is that the Father is the Father and the Son the Son. This becomes even more marked in Augustine's treatment, with his repeated apophaticism about the concept of the person, making clear his view that the concept is only used in order not to remain silent. The result is that the divine attributes are considered almost exclusively with respect to the doctrine of the one God; that all that is said of God's being is said of God as one, leaving the particular persons to languish in a kind of limbo.[1] In his treatment of the analogies Augustine

---

[1] Here, too, the parallel development in Pseudo-Dionysius is worth observing. See *The Divine Names* 2. 3–4 for the usual relentless stress on the unity of God, with the differentiations acknowledged but merely in terms of the illustrations of lights in a house which provide 'a single undifferentiated light'. Pseudo-Dionysius, *The Divine Names* 641A–C. The translation is from *Pseudo-Dionysius. The Complete Works*, translated by Colm Luibheid (London: SPCK, 1987), p. 61. The triune light is single, but it is differentiated, or, perhaps better, distributed between the three persons.

does attempt to show how the three persons of the Trinity might in some ways be conceived to parallel the three functions of the mind as memory, understanding and will, but disastrously, as one example will show. The characterization of the Spirit as 'love' and 'gift' – something Augustine appears to have inherited, at least in part, from Hilary of Poitiers[2] – appears, as we shall see, to apply more appropriately to the Father and the Son respectively. And Augustine's interpretation of the Son so largely in terms of Word, with its association with the eternal Platonic forms, is surely one of the reasons why the attributes of the Son are so heavily drawn from his eternal being rather than his action as incarnate.[3] In some ways this is understandable and inevitable, coming as it does at a time when the chief need was to defend the full and eternal divinity of the Son against Arianism and Sabellianism, that twin refusal to accept that the one who became incarnate is intrinsic to the being of divinity.

And yet even in Hilary, who is not so preoccupied as his successor with fitting the Son into the threefold scheme, it is what we might call the transcendent Christ rather than the one who has ascended bearing our humanity before the Father who is the almost sole object of attention. The Son is indeed all the things that Hilary attributes to him: the unbegotten, 'perfect from Him that is perfect',[4] the Word who was in the beginning, the mediator of creation, the life who is one with the Father eternally. As for Jesus' birth, it is its miraculous features that are stressed,[5] scarcely his

[2] Repeatedly in Hilary of Poitiers, *On the Trinity*, 2. 31–5. Augustine (*Trin.*, 6. 10. 11) attributes this conception to Hilary.

[3] I have set out evidence and argument for the interpretation, which remains controversial, in chapter 3 of *The Promise of Trinitarian Theology* (Edinburgh: T. & T. Clark, 2nd enlarged edition, 1997).

[4] Hilary, *Trinity*, 2. 11.

[5] Hilary, *Trinity*, 2. 27.

humanity. It is easy to hear Platonic undertones, if not
more, in the following: 'The inward reality is widely different from the outward appearance; the eye sees one thing,
the soul another.'[6] And before, turning to the Holy Spirit,
the following is said about the Lord's humanity. The paragraph is so short that it can be reproduced in full:

> So it was also during His further life on earth. The whole
> time which He passed in human form was spent upon the
> works of God. I have no space for details; it must suffice
> to say that in all the varied acts of power and healing
> which He wrought, the fact is conspicuous that He was
> man by virtue of the flesh He had taken, God by the
> evidence of the works He did.[7]

Now, the point is this. Hilary is speaking of the divine
Christ, the one called the second person of the Trinity, in a
treatise on the doctrine of God. The shortcoming is not in
that, but in the failure to draw on the human career of Christ
to characterize who he is *as divine*. We need to identify the
divine person by means of his human being if we are to
avoid positing a *logos asarkos* who is in some way conceived
independently of the human Jesus. Divinity is discussed in
the absence of the human story, which is precisely where
we should expect to find *what kind of divine person* we are
encountering.

And so Pannenberg is surely right in his remarks about
the outcome, that it means that talk of the being of the three

---

[6] Hilary, *Trinity*, 2. 27. Here is the beginning of the so-called
'christology from below', the method according to which one moves
from the human (in modern fashion, 'historical') Jesus to the divine
Christ (*per Christum hominem ad Christum deum!*); rather than
discerning, through the gift of the Spirit, the human Jesus *as also* the
divine Christ.

[7] Hilary, *Trinity*, 2. 28.

persons has come to be restricted to the relations of origin. All we can say of the eternal Son is that he is eternally begotten by the Father, of the Spirit that he proceeds from the Father (and possibly also from the Son). This is simply inadequate.

> When scripture bears witness to the active relations of the Son and Spirit to the Father, it is not good enough to treat these as not constitutive for their identity and in this respect to look only at the relations of begetting and proceeding (or breathing), viewing solely the relations of origin, which lead from the Father to the Son and Spirit, as applicable to the constitution of the persons.[8]

Before seeking a more adequate account of the particular being of the persons, one question should be adumbrated, to be answered in summary at the end of the section. Are persons, divine and human, univocally persons? As we have seen in Chapter 4 in particular, the question of the attributes is a question of the meaning of the words we use of the deity. When we use the word 'person' of God and the human being alike, do we use it with essentially the same meaning, or analogically? (It sometimes seems that the extremes of the negative theology make it appear that the usage is entirely equivocal.) One problem with analogy is, as we have seen in other cases, projection: we take what we believe to be characteristic of finite persons, and project this on to God by a process of denying what we take to be the marks of deficiency and elevating their supposedly positive features to infinity. Another is that the whole project of analogy is essentially Neoplatonist, in seeking to ascend a graded scale of being from lower to higher. That this

---

[8] Wolfhart Pannenberg, *Systematic Theology*, vol. 1, translated by G. W. Bromiley (Edinburgh: T. & T. Clark, 1991), p. 320.

process is no more satisfactory here than in the case of the attributes of the one God will appear when we have pursued a little further the problem of the relations of origin of the three persons of the godhead.

An approach to their identification in terms merely of relations of origin is not adequate to the way scripture speaks of the persons. But before giving some account of what scripture seems to suggest, let us recall the principle that has emerged from the previous chapters, that attributes are best spoken of in the closest possible relation to action. And if that is so, should we not expect that this will be the case with the particular persons also? Some of the Reformed dogmaticians were aware of the need to distinguish the persons in more respects than in their relations of origin, and so they are aware of the problem:

> [T]he three persons are distinct in name; in the order of their being, in the mode of their action, in their external effects; which indeed proceed from the entire Trinity, in which nevertheless the separate persons are active in a different way; and finally in the special attributes which belong to each person.[9]

The figures who tread the pages of Heppe's anthology are important for being aware not only of this necessity, but of its pitfalls too. Their treatment of the particular persons is prefaced with one of perichoresis.[10] Yet they are not aware

---

[9] Heinrich Heppe, *Reformed Dogmatics, Set out and Illustrated from the Sources*, translated by G. T. Thomson (Grand Rapids, Michigan: Baker, 1950), pp. 111–12.

[10] '... the completely close union, whereby one person is in another ... in the way in which every person permeates and embraces in every direction the whole of another always and inseparably ...', Heppe, *Reformed Dogmatics*, p. 113.

of the chief pitfall, which is the principle of *opera ad extra trinitatis sunt indivisa* (the actions of the Trinity outside are undivided), their conception of which effectively prevents them from distinguishing the forms of action of the distinct albeit inseparable persons. Their main attention continues to be given to the relations of origin, and when they come to the specific action they tend, like Barth after them, to distinguish in the wrong place, attributing creation to the Father, redemption to the Son and to the Spirit the motive power of the Father's and the Son's action in the world; or, alternatively, they distinguish them in terms of creation, redemption and sanctification.[11]

But that is to miss the point that, biblically speaking, all three of those actions are attributed to the Father and mediated by both the Son and the Spirit. The Father is the one who creates, reconciles, sanctifies, and the rest, but does so in every case by the actions of his two hands. The exponents of the approach to which objection is here being taken necessarily cannot distinguish between the different *kinds* of action of the three persons, and are, indeed, always in danger of modalism, for if to the Father is attributed creation, to the Son redemption and to the Spirit sanctification, there is always a temptation to attribute the unity of the divine action to some deity underlying the reality of Father, Son and Spirit. Rather, we need an account of the kind of person that the Father is in creating, redeeming and sanctifying – and anything else essential to an account of the economy of the divine action – and the kind of persons that the Son and the Spirit are in mediating that action as the Father's 'two hands' and therefore as the Father himself in action through their particular action. We need, that is to say, a distinction in terms of initiation and mediation rather

[11] Heppe, *Reformed Dogmatics*, pp. 115–32.

than of actions in the economy, which are indeed the work
of the whole Trinity, undivided certainly, but not homo-
geneous or monotonous. Let us begin with a text from
Paul, one moreover that appears to belong to an early form
of Christian confession.

'The grace (χάρις) of the Lord Jesus Christ and the love
(ἀγάπη) of God [the Father] and the fellowship (κοινωνία)
of the Holy Spirit . . .' (2 Cor. 13.14). There we have a
beginning, or rather the basis for a development. As other
passages of scripture suggest, and especially that passage to
which we continue to return, 1 John 4, love is not so much
appropriated to the Father as revealed to be his identifying
characteristic. This position gains some support from John
Zizioulas: 'A careful study of I John reveals that there . . .
the phrase "God is love" refers to the *Father*: the word
"God" is identified with Him who "sent his only-begotten
Son," etc.'[12] Love is that form of divine action which creates
the world, maintains it in face of sin and the Fall, acts for its
recreation in his Son and brings it finally to perfection
through the Spirit. The Father's action, mediated by the
Son and the Spirit, is love in action, bearing witness as it
does to the fact that God is *therefore* eternally love, love in
himself eternally, so that when God is eschatologically all
in all, love will be the final reality.

It is in this light that grace is shown to be the primary
characteristic of the Son, meaning the form of action
towards the world which the Son reveals and is. Grace is a
form, the form, of love in action. Jesus' love is the love of
God made known in action in the world, and paradigmatically in the love that goes to the cross for those who have

---

[12] John D. Zizioulas, *Being as Communion. Studies in Personhood
and the Church* (London: Darton, Longman and Todd, 1985), p. 46,
note 41.

made themselves unworthy of it. In face of sin and evil, grace takes the form of incarnational engagement with that which opposes God's love. Similarly, and revealingly, Jude 20f. distinguishes between the love of God and 'the mercy of our Lord Jesus Christ', implying a similar distinction between the first two persons of the Trinity. Like the love of God, grace and mercy can only be understood in terms of holiness, for it is a graciousness which takes the form of judgment – rejecting that which it must overcome – and appears to those who reject it as a threat. Yet, for all that it sometimes appears to be weakness and folly, it is a form of power, because it is empowered by the Spirit of the Father. To adopt Kierkegaard's expression, to which we shall return, it is the grace and power of God incognito, recognizable only to those to whom in the mystery of the divine acting it is revealed.

And that takes us to the third person, the Holy Spirit, whose form of action, in the churchly setting to which Paul's blessing belongs, is characterized as κοινωνία, communion, the form of relation between God and human beings that belongs to the final Kingdom but, in the time before the End, is realized only by the redemptive action of the Spirit. The Spirit's action is perfecting, eschatological action, realizing by anticipation that right relation between God and the creature and within created existence which is promised for the world to come. The Spirit makes holy: that is to say, makes things by anticipation what they will be when presented perfected before the throne of God the Father. The Spirit has to be understood in other eschatological respects, also. He is the Spirit of knowledge and understanding, enabling human minds to know something of the truth in anticipation of that time when we shall know as we are known. The stress on the gift of right understanding in those eschatological epistles of the church, Colossians and Ephesians, cannot be an accident. The Spirit, as we have seen in an earlier chapter,[13] is the Spirit of freedom, another eschatological reality, as we shall see if we consider also the non-human creation, that realm beyond and encompassing the human world. Here, the Spirit is the one who enables the whole creation to anticipate its eschatological destiny – 'liberated from its bondage to decay, and brought into the glorious freedom of the children of God' (Rom. 8.21) – enabling a measure of perfection there, too. This is especially, but by no means only, the case when men and women are enabled to fulfil their calling as those who, created in the image of God, behave in truly godlike fashion to the created world, enabling it to praise its maker as it was made to do.

In the preceding paragraphs, something has been sketched of the wider implications of the Pauline blessing. The Father is to be known particularly in terms of loving action, the Son in gracious, and, we might say, self-giving action, and the Spirit in the active creating of communion, broadening out into eschatological perfecting. This fulfils Pannenberg's requirement for active as well as passive roles for the Son and the Spirit. These forms of action show the persons to be distinct but not separate, and in that we return to the traditional doctrine that the divine attributes are all in a sense identical. To be gracious *is* to mediate the love of God, and to create communion between sinful human beings *is* to make that love real in the life of the church and, indeed, wherever there is genuine human fellowship. Yet it is also important to emphasize that while there is only one divine will – the perfection through redemption of the created

---

[13] Chapter 6, above, p. 105.

order – it is brought about by three persons or agents. In order to speak so, we must at the outset distinguish between person and individual. The three are not individuals, for none of their actions can be identified except as it takes place in relation to the other two. The Father creates through the Son and by the Spirit, while the Son does only what the Father gives him to do through the enabling Spirit and the Spirit is the eschatological and perfecting power and grace of God at work in the world through the Son. It remains the case, however, that if we fail to identify three distinct agents, we are not being true to the biblical witness.

That the Father is a particular personal agent seems to me not to need defence. He created the world, sent the Son and continues to send the Spirit through his Son to mediate his love to that world. So it is with the Son, who becomes incarnate and lives a fully human life of action and suffering in obedience to the Father's will. The Son is the subject of action in that he becomes incarnate, that is, in a particular mode of action *and therefore of being*. It is therefore simply not the case as has been suggested that either the Father or the Son or the Spirit could have become incarnate.[14] The Son alone is such because only he is eternally *incarnandus*, the one oriented to identification with those made in the image of God. He does what the Father gives him to do empowered by the Spirit, and that is how he is eternally and in the economy. He is an agent *because* the Father sends and the Spirit empowers. The Son as the one through whom the Father upholds the creation; the one who contains the creation within his creative power (the 'creative' cause), works in the world in ways suggested by Old Testament scripture and becomes incarnate in order through the Spirit's power to recreate the world which was

[14] Thomas Aquinas, *Summa Theologiae*, 3a. 3. 5.

threatened with a return to nothingness, as was famously expounded by Athanasius in the opening sections of *On the Incarnation of the Word*. To this end, he teaches, acts and takes the initiative in going to Jerusalem to suffer – a form of freely willed action, as we have seen. It is as such, as an authentically human agent, that he is the divine Son, although it seems to me that Pannenberg is attributing excessively autonomous, almost independent, agency to Jesus by speaking as he does of his *self*-distinction from the Father, rather than a distinction rooted in the Father's sending and the Spirit's empowering.[15] The Son's attributes are therefore those intrinsic to this form of action: as we have seen, holy and gracious action, both creating and redeeming.

But what of the Spirit? It is here especially that, bearing in mind that the Spirit is the *Father's* power in action – from Genesis 1.2 onwards – that we must avoid talk of *individual* – non-perichoretic – agency, because that is sometimes how people are heard to speak. The Spirit is neither an individual power nor a subjective feeling, but a person sent by the Father through his ascended Son. The problem accordingly is this. Can we move from Irenaeus' – and, it seems to me, scripture's – view of the Son and the Spirit as the 'two hands of God' – those who mediate the Father's action in the world – to what can be called a three-subject conception of the persons? (By 'subject' is meant one who is the subject of action; it need have no implication of conscious subjectivity, which is not what is at issue here.) In other words, does God the Father mediate his action through the

[15] Pannenberg, *Systematic Theology*, vol. 1, pp. 308–13. It is not that it is false to claim that Jesus distinguishes himself from the Father; it is rather doubtful whether this should form the principal defining mark of his being as the Son.

Son and Spirit without depriving them of their reality as *particular* agents, or does such a notion make them entirely passive? In the case of the Son, the matter seems to be this: the incarnate Son is truly an agent when he does the Father's will in the power of the Spirit. The Father, by sending his Spirit, enables him to be the authentic human being that he is. So it is with the Spirit, who is indeed sent through the Son, but is revealed in scripture as the one who acts as he does because the Father sends him. And he sends the Spirit as an agent: one who does things. Genesis 1.2 is, according to Basil, 'a sufficient proof for those who ask if the Holy Spirit took an active part in the creation of the world'.[16] The Spirit is an agent because he inspires prophecy, he teaches the truth, strengthens, encourages, and so on. The Spirit can be grieved and blasphemed, and enables decisions to be made not by excluding, but on the contrary by empowering human counsel: 'it seemed good to the Holy Spirit and ourselves'.

As the Father's power in action, accordingly, the Spirit is a subject and so variously active and passive in relation to the Father and to the world, and that includes, as we have seen, his relation to the incarnate Son, whose humanity he establishes by freeing him to be truly himself. The Spirit is the giver of life and of eternal life. Sanctifying – and perfecting more generally – is a form of action and therefore an attribute. This is not so much a matter of appropriating particular actions to the Father, Son and Spirit[17] as of bringing to the fore the distinctive forms of action of the persons each in relation to the other two: originating, becoming incarnate, perfecting. It is on this basis that we

[16] Basil, *Hex.*, 2. 6.
[17] This would risk a similar mistake to that involved in idealising or projectionist versions of the divine attributes.

must then speak of the Spirit as a person in the eternal
Trinity. On this account, centring as it does on the Spirit's
activity, he is not conceived as the bond of love between the
Father and the Son, but as the one who, in Basil's word's,
'completes the divine and blessed Trinity', serving not as
the one who completes an inward turning circle, but as one
who is the agent of the Father's outward turning to the
creation in his Son. As the one who 'completes', the Spirit
does indeed establish God's aseity, his utter self-sufficiency.
Yet this aseity is the basis of a movement outwards. So, to
return to our theme of the freedom given by the Spirit,
Robert Jenson sees this to be also the case in connection
with creation. 'The Spirit is *Spiritus Creator* as he frees the
Father from retaining all being with himself, and so frees
what the Father initiates from being the mere emanation it
would have been . . .'[18] The love of Father, Son and Spirit is
a form of love which does not remain content with its
eternal self-sufficiency because that self-sufficiency is the
basis of a movement outwards to create and perfect a world
whose otherness from God – of being distinctly itself – is
based in the otherness-in-relation of Father, Son and Spirit
in eternity.

And that leads us to tie in a remaining loose end. When
we speak of persons, divine and human, is 'person' being
used univocally? By this is meant not in exactly the same
sense, but recalling Scotus' view, that 'that concept [is]
univocal which possesses sufficient unity in itself, so that to
affirm and deny it of the same thing would be a contradiction'.[19] Persons are those particular beings – hypostases –
whose attributes are manifested in particular kinds of

[18] Robert W. Jenson, *Systematic Theology*, volume 1, *The Triune
God*; volume 2, *The Works of God* (New York and Oxford: Oxford
University Press, 1997, 1999), vol. 2, p. 26.
[19] Above, Chapter 4, note 20.

action, such as love, relationality, freedom, creativity. We have seen (above, Chapter 4) that the concept of love is used univocally of God's love and human love, because Jesus' love as human love is also the love of the Father in action. So it is with his person, which is, to repeat the NIV translation of Hebrews 1.3, 'the exact representation' of God's being. Jesus of Nazareth is the eternal Son of God, who *is* before Abraham *was*. What it is to be a human person is in this case identical with what it is to be a divine person, and therefore the word means the same at the levels of creator and creation.

II The 'Communication of Attributes'

The second problem to be treated in connection with the attributes of the particular persons of the Trinity is the doctrine of the *communicatio idiomatum* or communication of attributes, which holds that in some way or other the attributes of Christ's divine nature are communicated to the humanity, and – though usually less wholeheartedly – the reverse. The problems inherent in the topic are particularly evident in discussions arising from the Reformation, and appear in a different light in the Lutheran and Reformed traditions. Differences between the leading Reformers took shape in controversies not about christology itself so much as about its bearing on the doctrine of the Lord's Supper. Luther's concern to maintain the real presence of Christ in the bread and wine involved him in a strong doctrine both of the divinity of Christ and of the communication of attributes, a doctrine holding that anything predicated of Christ's divinity must also be predicable of his humanity, although the reverse was not at first taught (for example that the humanity's passibility implied that of the divine Word).[20] This teaching enabled Luther to argue that because divinity implies omnipresence, the human body of Christ could be present in the eucharistic elements by virtue of its participation in the divine nature. The outcome was that the Formula of Concord (1577) attributed to Christ's manhood the power of being present simultaneously in many places. This tendency to a total identification of the Word with the human flesh of Jesus increasingly came into difficulty as modern critical enquiry came to stress more strongly the humanity of Jesus, on the solid ground that the attribution of omnipotence and omniscience to the incarnate Word appeared to contradict the picture presented in the Gospels. The way out was sometimes sought in kenotic theory, according to which Christ, on becoming incarnate, was supposed either to suspend or to renounce those divine attributes which appeared to be inconsistent with his humanity.

On the Reformed side, the belief that humanity implied spatial location and therefore excluded omnipresence led to a different way of engaging the matter. Although Calvin's christology made more of the distinction between the divine and human natures, it was not Nestorian, and has recently been shown to owe much to that of Cyril of Alexandria.[21] The outcome of later debates, however, was that the natures were made to inhere in the person, so that ultimately, if not immediately, the attributes of the natures were located in the person of Christ. Heppe states what he takes to be the heart of the Reformed position as follows:

[20] It was only after Hegel's theology of the death of God that this became a truly live question.

[21] Bruce McCormack, *For Us and Our Salvation. Incarnation and Atonement in the Reformed Tradition* (Princeton: Princeton Theological Seminary, 1993), pp. 7–8.

Communicatio idiomatum . . . is that effect of the *unio personalis*, 'by which the attributes of each of the two natures coincide in one and the same person and are thereby also predicated of the person' (Mastricht V, iv, 12). For the attributes peculiar to either nature also belong to the person, because the natures have their substance in the person of Christ. Hence the attributes belong to the natures only *distincte*, whereas they belong to the person *indistincte*.[22]

There are in this traces of the treatment of the two natures almost as entities (*res*) that have to be balanced rather than as principles of Christ's being, and as a consequence Reformed christology has sometimes tended in a Nestorian direction. Aware of the problem, Bruce McCormack attempts the following solution, affirming first:

the principle that the two natures remain distinct and their properties unimpaired after the union. . . . Second . . . the language of 'subject' should not be used to translate *hypostasis* into a more modern idiom. The 'Subject' in this case is not the *hypostasis* as such, but the *hypostasis* together with the two natures that subsist in it.[23]

That will surely not do, because it turns properties, defining characteristics, into things. And that takes us to the problem that is intrinsic to the tradition, Catholic and Protestant alike, to treat natures as things which have attributes. But natures are not hypostases, and so do not have attributes; in a sense, they are attributes, ways of speaking of the fact that everything that Jesus does is both fully divine and fully

22 Heppe, *Reformed Dogmatics*, p. 439.
23 McCormack, *For Us and Our Salvation*, p. 16.

human action.[24] The person who acts is the eternal Son of God, become truly human without loss of his divinity.

As Schleiermacher saw, much depends on the concept of nature with which this matter is construed. His famous discussion of the problems of the two-nature doctrine, however, makes a number of points, whose assumptions will take us to the heart of our problem. One is that the word 'nature' should not be used indifferently of the divine and the human, because God and man are by it classified under one and the same universal. Nature, he holds, implies corporeality and limitedness, while God is necessarily uncompound and absolutely simple. But this is not compatible, Schleiermacher holds, with an adequate account of the person of Christ:

> For in utter contradiction to the use elsewhere, according to which the same nature belongs to many individuals or persons, here one person is to share in two quite different natures. Now if 'person' indicates a constant unity of life, but 'nature' a sum of ways of actions or laws, according to which conditions of life vary and are included within a fixed range, how can the unity of life coexist with the duality of natures, unless the one gives way to the other . . . or unless they melt into each other . . .?[25]

If one begins with a priori definitions of what it is to be divine and what it is to be human, it is scarcely surprising that the doctrine leads into difficulties. Much depends upon

[24] Natures do not do things, but express the whatness, *quidditas* of entities.

[25] F. D. E. Schleiermacher, *The Christian Faith*, translated by H. R. Mackintosh and J. S. Stewart (Edinburgh: T. & T. Clark, 1928), p. 393. The preceding exposition is a summary of some of the points from pp. 392–4.

what is meant in speaking of 'nature' as a sum of ways or actions or laws. If to be divine is to be omnipotent and omniscient, and God is defined a priori as 'uncompound and absolutely simple', then Jesus must, apparently, be so; yet it appears that to be human is precisely not to possess these attributes, so that almost any doctrine of the *communicatio* leads into apparently insuperable difficulties, as the history of the so-called kenotic christology only too well witnesses.

However, if the attributes of the Son are first of all derived from his incarnate condition – from the act of becoming man and living a human life – then we shall be concerned not primarily with omnipotence etc., but with the eternal Son's capacity to become man without loss of his divinity. Here Schleiermacher's dismissal of 2 Peter 1.4, which addresses its readers as being in receipt of promises through which they may be participants in the divine nature (θείας κοινωνοὶ φύσεως), is instructive. '[I]t is hardly to be denied', Schleiermacher writes, 'that this expression, if we go back to the original Greek word, bears in itself traces of heathen influence, though possibly of unconscious influence.'[26] Such an observation comes ill from one who himself appears to have accepted a traditional definition of God bearing more than a little of 'heathen influence, though possibly of unconscious influence'. Indeed, we might ask how far his whole discussion of the natures depends on an assumption, deriving from the Enlightenment's essentially Hellenic critique of Christian theology, that God and man are opposed rather than ontologically distinct realities.

It will be more than instructive if we subject the verse from 2 Peter also to the kind of contextual analysis which

---

[26] Schleiermacher, *The Christian Faith*, p. 393.

did so much in earlier chapters to undermine the support of scripture for the negative theology. The broader context of the passage in 2 Peter 1 is not eschatological nor indeed to do with 'sharing the life of God' except in a strongly this-worldly sense.[27] The injunction to 'escape the corruption in the world caused by evil desires' is glossed by a list of what can only be called the virtues: goodness, knowledge, self-control, perseverance, godliness, brotherly kindness, love, all of them forms of faithful action which 'will keep you from being unproductive in your knowledge of our Lord Jesus Christ'. And that in turn takes us to one of the dictionary definitions of nature (φύσις) as referring to 'the natural powers, constitution or condition of a thing', in Schleiermacher's terms, 'a sum of ways of actions or laws'. To share the divine nature is therefore to live in the world after the manner of the eternal Son of God made man. It is thus precisely parallel to the Johannine instruction that we must love as God has loved us. It is from there that we have to infer what it is for Jesus to have divine and human 'natures'. We cannot decide what they are simply a priori, but have to ask what they are in the case of the particular divine and human action which encounters us here.

And action, as with all the attributes, is at the heart of the matter. Barth has rightly suggested that we should speak not so much of a communication of idioms as of a communication of graces or operations.[28] It might be clearer if we

---

[27] This is a disputable interpretation, especially in that it requires taking 'escape the corruption of the world' not in an eschatological sense, but to be glossed in verses 5–9 as its opposite. That is, the whole passage refers to the Christian life in the world, the eschatological note coming only in verses 10–11. I am grateful to Eddie Adams for discussion of this passage.

[28] Karl Barth, *Church Dogmatics*, translation edited by G.W. Bromiley and T. F. Torrance (Edinburgh: T. & T. Clark, 1957–1975), 4/2, pp. 75–89, 104–12.

concentrate on the notion of action. The human acts of Jesus are at the same time and without confusion the acts of the eternal Son of God, and *therefore* the humanly mediated acts of God the Father, because Jesus *is* the eternal Son of God. That makes it possible to give an account of one attribute, that of omnipresence. It has never been suggested that the human Jesus is omnipresent, although, as we have seen, his ascended humanity has notoriously been so described in some Lutheran theology. But if, along with Barth, we construct the doctrine not abstractly but on the basis of this particular presence of the Son to the world – from the Father and by the Spirit – what we discover is the incarnation as an expression of God's capacity to be present to the world – anywhere and everywhere – on the basis of what we know of his particular presence in Jesus. Thus while Jesus is not omnipresent, his life is the taking place of the capacity of the creator of time and space to be freely present to it. We might say the same about omnipotence. Jesus is not, as incarnate, omnipotent; but his life is the expression of God the Father's omnipotent dealing with his creation through the life and death of his incarnate Son. That is to say, we take with absolute seriousness (univocally?) Paul's claim in 1 Corinthians 1.24 that the crucified Christ is the power and the wisdom of God, the Father's attributes in action.

III *Unknowability Again*

It should not be supposed that a final solution to all the problems of the doctrine of the attributes will be achieved simply by an appeal to the notion of action, but it seems to me beyond doubt that some of the antinomies and offences

bequeathed to the tradition by the paganizing of the doctrine of God will become less insuperable. This brief study
has been designed chiefly to create an awareness of the
rift in the tradition and to suggest alternative ways of
approaching the doctrine. The book began with a critique
of the negative theology, and an argument that its predom-
inance in the tradition owes more to the Presocratic and
Platonic critique of the pagan gods than one which would
take its orientation from scripture. Theologically, a large
part of the error this tendency creates is a denial of
the knowability of God which paradoxically conceals a
Promethean 'hidden agenda': to achieve unity with the
divine apart from the mediation of the Father by the Son
and the Spirit.

Against this, it has been argued that we should take with
utter seriousness that the Holy Spirit enables us to know
the Father through Jesus, who is the eternal Son of the
Father made man. This means two things. First, it follows
that the negative way should be rejected absolutely, because
it takes the form of an ascent out of the creation to a God
who is essentially its opposite rather than its other-in-
relation. Second, it follows that we do not need first to
ascend from the material to the immaterial beyond because
the Son of God has already taken up his dwelling among us,
as Jesus of Nazareth. We might almost take as a text here
Paul's words in Romans 10:

> Do not say in your heart, 'Who will ascend into heaven?'
> (that is, to bring Christ down) or 'Who will descend into
> the abyss?' (that is, to bring Christ up from the dead).

In its various forms, the approach rejected by the apostle is the project of the negative way. But Jesus Christ has already been raised from the dead and ascended into heaven, whence the Father has through him sent the Holy Spirit, the Spirit of truth and the source of human knowledge of the Father, ruling out attempts to bypass or relativize the trinitarian route.

> But what does it say? The word is near to you, on your lips and in your heart (that is, the word of faith which we preach). (Rom. 10.6–8)

The negative way is essentially a form of unbelief, seeking God prior to and other than through the incarnation and sending of the Spirit. We might say the same of the whole programme known as analogy, because it is tied up with it. Because we fail to realize that the (human) love that Jesus is is at the same time the love of God in action, we fail to accept the univocal language which it licenses, indeed, requires, and seek instead a form of language that effectively ignores the means given.

In conclusion, two points should be made. The first comes from Luther's diatribe against that exponent of the negative way, Erasmus of Rotterdam. Luther's insistence on the knowability of God derives from a most practical concern:

> if I am ignorant of what, how far, and how much I can and may do in relation to God, it will be equally uncertain and unknown to me, what, how far, and how much God can and may do in me, although it is God who works everything in everyone. . . . But when the works and power of God are unknown, I do not know God

himself, and when God is unknown, I cannot worship, praise, thank and serve God, since I do not know how much I ought to attribute to myself and how much to God.[29]

It is important to note that Luther is here referring not simply to the economy of God's action, but to God in himself, for like all the best theologians he knows that God's historic action is God the Father himself in action. 'If you teach us to talk such nonsense about God, and are so set against the locating of his essence, you will end by not even allowing him to remain for us in heaven . . .'[30] To be a Christian, therefore, is to make assertions; indeed to live by them:

> For it is not the mark of a Christian mind to take no delight in assertions; on the contrary, a man must delight in assertions, or he will be no Christian.
>
> I am speaking, moreover, about the assertion of those things which have been transmitted to us in the sacred writings.[31]

Luther's fundamental conviction is that scripture makes God known, and we know that it does because God raised Jesus from the dead:

> For what still sublimer thing can remain hidden in the Scriptures, now that the seals have been broken, the

[29] *Luther: on the Bondage of the Will*, translated by Philip S. Watson, *Luther and Erasmus: Free Will and Salvation*, Library of Christian Classics, vol. 17 (London: SCM Press, 1969), p. 117. I am grateful to Robert Jenson for pointing me to this wonderful passage.

[30] *Luther: on the Bondage of the Will*, p. 126.

[31] *Luther: on the Bondage of the Will*, p. 105.

stone rolled from the door of the sepulcher . . ., and the supreme mystery[32] brought to light, namely that Christ the Son of God has been made man, that God is three and one, that Christ has suffered for us and is to reign eternally?[33]

The second and culminating observation is that the moments of truth of the doctrine of divine unknowability should not be denied. The finite mind, and certainly the sinful mind, may not of its own powers know the essence of God. That becomes possible only on God's terms: by the atoning death of Christ and the appropriation of reconciliation with God by the act of the Spirit. But that very reality implies that God is knowable, because he makes himself known. Again and again the Gospels – and especially John's Gospel – and the Epistles offer us knowledge, and, indeed, recommend its necessity: knowledge of 'the Father, from whom his whole family in heaven and on earth derives its name' (Eph. 3.15). But that knowledge is in God's gift, not a natural human capacity of the kind that thinks it can achieve a mystical knowledge of God apart from Christ by means of negative theological projection. For at its heart is the fact that God is knowable through the strait and narrow gate that is the humanity of Christ, as narrated in scripture and proclaimed in the church. He really is a human being, and can be recognized to be also and at the same time the eternal Son of God only through the Spirit. ('Flesh and blood has not revealed this to you, Peter, but my Father in heaven', Matt. 16.17.)

The man Jesus of Nazareth, crucified, risen and seated at the right hand of God still clothed in his humanity, is, to use

[32] And we recall our discussion of this word in chapter 5 above, p. 92.
[33] *Luther: on the Bondage of the Will*, p. 110.

an expression of Karl Barth's, albeit in rather a different way, the knowability of God on our side.[34] Instead, therefore, of speaking of God's unknowability – a pagan form of unbelief – we should speak rather of his incognito. The Son of God comes as one who 'had no beauty or majesty to attract us to him, nothing in his appearance that we should desire him. He was despised and rejected of men, a man of sorrows and familiar with suffering' (Isa. 53.2–3). We cannot evade that narrow road along which we must pass if we are to know the God and Father of our Lord Jesus Christ. And yet we must gloss Isaiah's poem, for this man who had nothing 'in his appearance' that we should desire him, is in fact that beauty and majesty of God in action. In that incognito we truly find the attributes of our God, for there is God in action, in the richness of his utter simplicity.

[34] Karl Barth, *Church Dogmatics*, 2/1, p. 150.

Index